The TRUTH ABOUT Us

How to Discover the Potential God has Given You

Author: Mable C. Dunbar, Ph.D.
Copy editor: Jeri Lyn Rogge and Joyce Jesse
Cover design: Palimor Studios
Manager & Layout designer: Kristi Chevalier

For additional copies:
Advent*Source*
5040 Prescott Avenue
Lincoln, NE 68506
(800) 328-0525
www.adventsource.org

Revised 2004 by
Advent*Source*

ISBN# 1-57756-095-7

Printed in the U.S.A.

Table of Contents

Dedication

To my mother, Ellen Douglas, thank you for allowing me to be born.

To my friend, Polly Westman, thank you for supporting and believing in me.

To my friend, Cynthia Prime, thank you for challenging me never to give up on my dreams.

Acknowledgment

To my husband Colin, thank you for faithfully loving me, believing in me, and creating a safe environment whereby I can use and expand my spiritual gifts. You are God's gift to me.

To my children: Elrene, Elizabeth and Colin, Jr., You are the apple of my eye and continue to give me joy.

To friends and mentors who encourage, support, motivate, and appreciate me: Elizabeth Sterndale, Rose Otis, Madlyn Hamblin, Deborah Harris, Jean Parchment, Linda Schultz, Lenore Brantly, Carole Kilcher, Kit Watts, Margaret Poole, and Peggy Cain. You might not know it, but you have impacted my life in very special ways.

To special men who help me learn how to value male friendships: Wendell Simons, Michael Fields (deceased), Philip Prime, Ron Westman, Rick Kosinski, Don Wilson, Jerry Kantor, and Clinton Schultz.

To Daddy (Ivan Douglas), for loving and accepting me in spite of it all.

To my family members, you know who I am and love me just the same.

To Peggy Foster, you have been my loyal friend and secretary for over 10 years. There have been hard times, yet you always support me and encourage me by your loyalty so that I never gave up. I appreciate you.

To Jean Illsey Clarke, author of Self Esteem: A Family Affair who taught me affirmations, how to affirm others, and the importance of affirmations.

To the board, staff, advisors, and volunteers of Women In Renewal, Inc. (Polly's Place, Mary's Inn, The Renewal Institute). You have demonstrated commitment and patience as we develop and expand the agency to address issues relating to domestic violence in religious circles.

To Mary Maxson and the other dynamic women who direct and coordinate Women's Ministries organizations and minister on behalf of other women, families and churches, you have given and continue to give me the opportunity to conduct retreats, seminars, and workshops in your churches and communities.

To the church leaders, officers, and members who utilize their time, efforts and funds to assist the hurting.

To the administration of the Upper Columbia Conference for verbally and financially endorsing efforts to assist individuals dealing with abuse issues within religious circles. (From the writer's perspective, they are the first administrative leaders in the Seventh-day Adventist Church to express their burden to develop a healing center for their hurting constituents, and financially support efforts to make the center a reality).

To my clients, you have demonstrated your trust in me by sharing your pain, life stories, dreams, challenges, and triumphs as you journey towards recovery and renewal. You have added richness and dimension to my life. Your struggles have been my struggles. Your pain has been my pain. Your joys have been my source of inspiration and determination to do the ministry God has called me to do.

To GOD: Thank you for empowering me to be alive
to be uniquely me
to think and feel,
and do.

Introduction

Dear Reader:

As a therapist, I have discovered that many of my clients base their thoughts, actions, and feelings about themselves on what other people told/tell them about their being and potential. Through the years I have recognized that negative messages can impact an individual to such an extent that he or she can become emotionally, socially, mentally, and spiritually crippled.

The purpose of this manual is to help you affirm yourself as a unique individual. I hope that as you read and reflect on your being and journey through life, you will realize the potential God has given you. I hope that its contents will empower, encourage and inspire you to live an abundant and fruitful life because of who you are: a wonderful and powerful creation of the Almighty.

If while reading or doing the exercises you feel overwhelmed, anxious, fearful, or angry, seek help from a professional counselor or trusted, caring friend. It is okay to share your thoughts and feelings with a safe person.

I tell my story at the beginning of each chapter because I want you to know that I understand some of the dysfunctional thoughts, feelings and behaviors you have had because of what others might have said about you or done to you. My road to triumph started when I found strength and purpose to my life in the realization and acceptance of the fact that God loves me and wants to use me for His glory. I have decided to live for Him knowing that He will strengthen me to do His will. He will take care of me. Therefore, I never need to be afraid of anything or anyone.

In each chapter you will find ways in which we limit ourselves, undeniable facts about who we are and what we can do, positive messages that we can claim and memorize, and affirmations from the Bible to rehearse instead of the negative messages that might be playing over and over in your mind.

In each chapter there are exercises that I encourage you to do in order to put into practice what you read. Then you will find true stories about individuals who found triumph in recognizing their value to God. Their names and other identifying situations have been changed to protect their identity. I hope that the poems and positive messages from the Bible will encourage you to value your specialness to God. Bible messages are taken from The Clear Word.

I have done my best to give credit for any work that I have cited. If for some reason, the author has not been credited, please let me know so that I can make corrections in future publications.

Finally, there is a list of books that I have read and found helpful in my quest for recovery and renewal. If you choose to read them, I hope that they will be helpful to you too. Continue to read and attend workshops and seminars. This manual is not intended to take the place of a professional counselor. Get professional assistance if there is a need. Good Christian counselors are out there: search until you find one. Put into practice any new ideas or skills you find helpful. You owe it to God and yourself to grow and thrive and thrive you will because His love is in you and with you. If you choose, nothing will separate you from that love.

> I am convinced that nothing can force its way between us and Christ, whether it's life or death, angels or earthly powers or forces in the universe, things present or things to come, heights or depths, or any living being you can name, because God's love for us is made manifest by our redemption through Jesus Christ our Lord" Romans 8:38, 39.

As we claim the promises of God and hold fast to the truth of our inestimable value to Him, together we will triumph. You are loved!

Mable Dunbar Ph.D.

CHAPTER ONE

The Right to Be

"We are, because God is" Swedenborg.

He watched me every day as I walked by his home from school. I was 14 years old. This day he decided that he would approach me. He told me that he had noticed me for a while and wanted to talk with me.

"Would that be alright with you?"

"Sure."

Then he led me down a steep hill behind his friend's home. Why did I go? I don't know. I had no reason to fear him. He seemed nice enough. When we reached his destination, he asked me if I would consider being his girlfriend. I had no clue what being a girlfriend meant, except that we would do things together and I would have someone to talk to.

"Sure," I said.

Then he asked me to kiss him.

Immediately a feeling of horror and panic engulfed me. I was frightened. I almost felt powerless. I could not explain my feelings, but I pushed him aside and ran up the hill to the safety of my home. I was angry with myself. I knew that I could not and should not trust men. Why was I so gullible to believe that he would actually like me rather than what he thought he might get from me? Why did I let any boy get so close to me?

I knew that I was different from other girls because of what people told me about my birth and how they treated me. I was an illegitimate child, a product of rape. Well-meaning Christians (especially older women) did not know how to relate to me. Even though they knew I had nothing to do with the nature of my birth, they could not view me as "normal." I was "soiled." They gave me subtle messages about who I was and what I could or could not do. These messages told me I was not entitled to the same privileges as other children. I should not expect or strive for the best. I had limitations.

I grew up feeling that I was not good enough, that I did not belong, that I did not fit in with any group. I believed that my existence was accidental. I began to wonder what purpose was there to my life. I tried hard to please everyone, because in doing so, I thought I would be valued. I worked hard for validation as a human being, as a woman. I fooled myself into believing that if I labored hard in the church, and do all the right things: sing, play the piano, hold offices, attend every service, I would be worthy of life in spite of my "unplanned," "unwanted," and "illegitimate" birth. The feelings of inadequacy limited my being for many years.

HOW WE LIMIT OUR RIGHT TO BE

We protect scared self by being angry or depressed.

Rather than deal with our anger in constructive ways, we lash out at those we feel do not understand us, reject us, or might appear not "like" us. We are timid and afraid to express our fear, we crawl into a shell and focus so much on ourselves that we lack the energy or motivation to perform. We become depressed and lose hope. Without hope, life has little or no meaning.

We avoid pain or hide our fear by appearing powerful, controlling, strong, or cold.

We give the impression that we are in control, that we have it all together, that we are able to handle any situation, so that others will not know how fearful we really are. By appearing powerful or cold, they will not approach or disagree with us. We hope to be protected from their attacks so that they will not be able to hurt us.

We try to get others to do for us what we can do for ourselves.

We do not want people to leave us. We want them to care for us. We want their sympathy and support. Therefore, we do not let them know that we have certain skills or talents because if they realized that we could do for ourselves, they might feel that we do not need them. They might abandon us and not give us the attention we desperately crave.

We do for others to get validation for being.

We sometimes do for other people, even if we don't want to. We need them to assure us that we are important because of what we have to offer or what we can do. It is our hope that they will make us feel good about ourselves so that their perception of us will give us value and self-worth.

We act scared or incompetent to keep people close to us.

We perform in ways that are not consistent with our gifts and talents. We give the impression that we "can't" or don't know how. We hope that this will keep them from abandoning and rejecting us.

We act aloof for fear of being known.

If people do not know who we are, understand our capabilities, or don't have any expectations of us, we cannot fail or disappoint them. As a result, we don't get involved. We become spectators.

AFFIRMATION OF OUR RIGHT TO BE

Fact:
We have the right to be alive.

Message:
God meant for me to be alive. If He didn't, I wouldn't be here.

Affirmation:
"I praise You, for this body is incredibly and wonderfully made. Your whole creation is a marvel, and I know that it all didn't just happen. When I was developing in my mother's womb, nothing took place that You didn't know. To You there is nothing secret and mysterious. You saw my unformed body inside the womb. You knew how long I would live even before I was born" Psalm 140:14-16.

Handwrite the message and affirmation. Place it on your mirror, refrigerator or somewhere you will see it regularly.

"In Him I live and move and have my being, which makes me His offspring" Acts 17:28 (last part).

Fact:
We have the right to belong.

Message:
It does not matter how my family of origin treated me; I can be part of a family or a group of people who will appreciate, love, value, and make me feel secure. I need to explore until I find them.

Affirmation:
"You have helped me along life's path. I feel secure in Your presence as if I were under Your wings. I want to stay close by Your side because You keep me safe" Psalm 63:7.

Fact:

We have the right to be happy.

Message:

There are disappointments in life. There are times that I will be sad, discontent, and hurt. But I will experience more times to be grateful, and optimistic because pain will not last forever. I will count my blessings and be joyful. I will remind myself that happiness comes from within. I will start being happy about the fact that I am created in God's image and that He cares for me, and rejoices over me.

Affirmation:

"The Lord my God is in my midst. He is with me and is strong to save. He delights in me and will quiet me with His love. He will rejoice over me with singing" Zephaniah 3:17.

Fact:

We have the right to take care of ourselves.

Message:

No one really understands me as much as God does. Because I am important to God, I will take care of His investment, ME. I will be sure to utilize whatever will keep my mind, body, and spirit renewed and revived. I will lovingly release old negative patterns and negative images of myself that keep me from valuing who I am.

Affirmation:

"I have been bought with a price which no human can pay. Therefore, I will honor the One who paid the price for me, because now I belong to Him" 1 Corinthians 6:20.

Fact:

We have the right to be healthy.

Message:

I will eat the right foods for me, exercise the best way for me, and trust Him to tell me what is best for me. I will take care of my marvelous body that is uniquely mine and keep it in such a way that I can be proud of it.

Affirmation:

"Dear____________________(supply your name)

Above everything else, I want things to go well with you and for your body to be as healthy as your soul." 3 John 2.

Fact:

We have the right to be treated with dignity and respect.

Message:

I will not allow others to treat me disrespectfully. I will respect myself because I was carefully and marvelously made. I will be compassionate and gracious to myself. I will remember that when I am dignified and respectful of myself, I am teaching others to treat me the same way.

Affirmation:

"I will express my gratitude to God, the Father of our Lord Jesus Christ, who is most gracious and compassionate towards me and who is the God of all comfort" 2 Corinthians 1:3.

Fact:

We have the right to honor our value system as it is ordained by God and appropriate for us.

Message:

It is important for me to take time to identify and solidify my values. I will not allow anyone to deter me from living by those principles that will help me achieve my goals and become a better person for the Lord. Even if others don't agree with me, that's okay because I can decide what I want and need, with God's help. This does not mean that my values cannot change. I have the right to decide when, how, where, and why I need to change them based upon my comfort level, convictions, and commitment to change. I will honor my values. In honoring my values, I am honoring myself.

Affirmation:

"You made me only a little lower than angels, to minister to others as they do. You even honored me by sharing part of Your creative power and glory with me" Psalm 8:5.

Fact:

We have the right to say no to anything when we feel we are not ready for it, it is unsafe, or if it violates our well being. We have the right to feel scared and to say, "I am afraid." "That does not feel comfortable to me."

Message:

I will not allow anyone to force me to do something that I am not ready to do. Sometimes my inner voice tells me that I am not safe. I need to trust that voice and get out of the situation immediately without arguing with myself. I must remember that my life is a priority. I will not allow anyone or anything to make me feel that my choice to protect myself is a bad one.

Affirmation:

"As I trust what You say and follow through on it, I will shout for the joy it brings to my heart. You will defend and protect me. And I will be grateful and love You all the more. Lord, I know You bless those who love and obey You. Your love surrounds them like a shield" Psalm 6:11, 12.

Fact:

We have the right to be in a non-abusive environment even if we displease others.

Message:

I hear many voices: my family, my church, my school, my friends, and society, telling me what I should or should not do. That I should make sure to do nothing to cause confusion, bring dishonor to God, or break up my family. Yet I am being hurt, humiliated, and destroyed. Will I bring dishonor to God if I protect His treasure, His investment? ME! If I allow myself to stay in an abusive situation, am I not condoning the violence? Am I not allowing my abuser to perfect his/her dysfunctional character? Staying in an abusive situation will only make me vulnerable for more abuse. Therefore, I need to take action to avoid continued victimization.

Affirmation:

"Then Jesus straightened up and said to the woman who was still trembling in fear, expecting to hear her sentence of doom, 'Where are all those who were accusing you? It looks like they've gone. There is no one here to condemn you.' She looked around and said, 'You're right, Lord. There's not a one.' Jesus responded, 'Neither am I going to condemn you. You're forgiven. You may go now, but leave your life of sin'" John 8:11, 12.

Fact:

You have the right to establish healthy relationships.

Message:

When I am unhealthy it is challenging to establish relationships with healthy people. But I can. There are individuals who are well in the process of their recovery. They know who they are, where they are going, and rely on God to help them get there. And as they journey, they will nurture me. They will inspire, encourage, and empower me to grow. These are the kinds of relationships that I can pursue and rely on.

Affirmation:

"There is no greater way to show love for a friend than to give your life for her/him" John 15:13.

"I have never treated you like servants and I never will. Servants aren't told everything their masters are planning to do. But you're my friends …" John 15:15.

DOORS, WINDOWS, AND CRACKS

Janice's Story

I am the youngest of three children. My brother is eight years older and my sister is six years older. We grew up in the Northwest corner of Chicago in a "blue collar" ethnic neighborhood of Italian, Polish, Irish and German descent. I was raised in a Catholic environment going to parochial schools from first grade through high school. I did attend a Catholic college and am the only college graduate in my family.

My father was a business salesperson and had a drinking and gambling problem. My mother concealed these problems and became co-dependent, covering up my father's omissions or mistakes. I was constantly seeking attention, but it was not easy to come by given the dynamics of an alcoholic household. I observed that if I wanted something I had to do it myself. I didn't trust authority figures and became a little adult myself. My father was very loving and kind but when he drank he was another person whom I feared and didn't understand. My Mom always denied his illness with alcohol and gambling.

She grew up in an alcoholic family and so did my father. He was raised by his mother and grandmother who were very supportive and loving to him. He always longed to have a relationship with his father but it was forbidden. My mother was raised by both of her parents and she was quite an independent person. During the war, she enrolled in the women's air corp which was very assertive for women of her time.

As a child, I was very smart and observant. I talked about what I saw happening around me but was told to "keep my mouth shut and don't talk about your Dad's drinking and gambling." I was told that things didn't happen when they actually did. This distorted reality was very detrimental in my later life during an abusive marriage. I didn't believe what was occurring, instead I pretended that things didn't happen or it would get better.

At the age of 18 I left to go to college at the discouragement of my parents (both my brother and sister dropped out and they feared that I would do the same and waste more of their money in the process). I wanted to escape my roots of "blue collar" life and become a successful person, a lawyer or someone who made lots of money.

I met my future husband the second week of college and we started our 15 year relationship. At this time both of us were involved in lots of drinking and drugs. We both were very competent people who wanted to escape our family lives. He grew up in the inner city. He was the eldest of two and was very bright, the top of his class. He was studying to be a chemist just like his deceased father had been. His father was vice president of a chemical company and died of a massive heart attack three years earlier at the age of 38. After his father's death, he assumed all responsibilities of a man 20 year his senior. His mother was very dominant, and he was expected to serve her needs and wants. Each day he would prepare dinner for his mother and younger brother who was just 13 months younger. Additionally he was like a "husband" to her. They discussed matters that affected the household and his younger brother was treated like a child.

All he wanted was to escape the responsibility of being an adult and have fun. All I wanted was to be "intelligent" and move away from my "blue collar" roots. When we met there was an understanding between us. He would take care of me, help me to learn and achieve good grades, I would care for him, laugh with him and party with him. We never did much thinking about anything different, but grades, partying and having fun. I did pull away from my "blue collar" friends and changed. Luckily my friends cared about me during these 15 years and reached out to me throughout this time. My friends were with me during the breakup and divorce. These friends were my only sense of who I was and they reminded me who I would be when I was breaking away from him. I am forever grateful to them.

I was attracted to my husband because he was very intelligent, responsible, hard-working and going to be a great scientist one day. He told me that once he got into the harder courses I would have to draw upon the past and believe in our relationship. The most important thing in his life was science and succeeding. I was important but not the primary thing. The abuse began when I wanted to become a lawyer. I told him I would be sitting in for my last exam and he blew up at me. He didn't want to be married to a "career woman." He didn't want to be with someone who wouldn't be at home to raise children, etc. (Later he told me he never wanted children and refused to support my attempts to get an advanced degree). He became verbally abusive and threatened me when I began to work. He criticized my work attire, meetings I had to attend after 5:00 p.m., and would sabotage my success by either not recognizing my achievements or belittling them. My self-esteem at home was fragile.

When I went to work I became "superwoman." I worked hard for recognition and was worthy of promotion. The problem was relocation and he would not hear of it. I subjugated my career endeavors and sabotaged my success time after time. It was like climbing to the top of a mountain, getting to the peak, enjoying the sunlight, then tossing myself off the peak under a boulder and trying to work my way back up again. I began to drink to ease the pain and developed an addition to alcohol. We would be drinking buddies and this was the only time he would be gentle or nice. He was a sweet drunk.

Finally, after two moves across the country to chase after his career dreams, we settled into a small town in Michigan. It was here that I found myself, some help and recognized the relationship and how unhealthy it had been. It took me 4 years to become aware and gradually build my self-esteem (lost weight, cut my hair, got new clothes, and found Jesus). I recognized that I had a drinking problem and told my husband that I was going to seek help. He laughed, then he got angry and threatened me. I became more aware of the emotional abuse he was dishing out to me, began to call it to his attention and told him I would no longer take it. He became angry and started to squeeze me really tight and shake me or corner me in a room and yell at me. Finally, I was worried about my safety and planned to leave the house. I called a shelter for abused women and made a plan to re-establish credit in my own name, got a post office box of my own, and looked for an apartment. He became violent and scared me. So I waited until he had a business trip, packed up my things and left him a letter. In it I told him that this was the most difficult decision I ever made for myself. I needed to be safe and sober and begin to live my life for me.

During this time the Lord was guiding my path and opening doors, windows and cracks for me to go through. I told my husband I would only meet him at a therapist's office or a very public place with a friend. He lost it and pleaded for me to return. Then he became angry when I would not and threatened to divorce me. He called all my relatives and told them I was having a nervous breakdown. Some of them actually believed him. I was solid, sober and began to look at things differently, more peaceful, more serene, more present.

We divorced nine months later. It was a bitter divorce. He would not part with my personal things and held them until the divorce was final. I prayed during this time for the Lord to provide me strength and safety, and to forgive him for his anger. I prayed that he would find peace. In the end it was me who came out ahead.

I've got my life back and am working toward becoming a Doctor of Osteopath. I am just two courses away from taking the medical school entrance exams. I am proud of my accomplishments of getting all A's in my chemistry courses, contrary to my husband saying that I would be a failure and never learn science. He was threatened by me. I am smart and always was. I just needed to apply myself. As for my "blue collar" friends, they have welcomed me back with open arms and they have said that they're grateful to have the "old" me back. I had been lost for 15 years.

I can truly say I have it all: my life, my career, goals, Jesus, my true friends and my sanity and peace. There are days when I ask "Did I do the right thing?" Then I remember my former self waking up from an alcoholic blackout, looking at my lifeless image in the mirror. Yes, I did make the right decision!

My message to other victims is to keep yourself safe and work on yourself first. Even with children, you must take care of your needs. Then you can help others. The hardest step is the first one to making change. God has a path for each of our lives and it was meant to shine His good works for all to see. The only way to do this is to be true to yourself and honest with others.

It's never too late to go after your dreams. All you need is to believe that you are worthy and pray to God to show you the doors, windows and cracks to walk through. It's up to you to walk once God provides the path.

SOME CHARACTERISTICS OF A TRUSTED FRIEND OR HELPER

As you read the stories and do the exercises in this book you may find it helpful to have have a trusted friend that you can confide in. Here are some important characteristics you should look for in a trusted friend or helper.

Available

Your helper will be willing and able to find the time to assist you. They are not too preoccupied with their own issues that they do not have quality time to concentrate on you and your concerns.

Non-Judgmental

They will not misrepresent or misinterpret you or force their opinions on you. They will be objective in helping you find solutions to your problems rather than condemn you for not "doing the right thing."

Trustworthy & Confidential

He or she will be responsible to you and not divulge any of your confidences. They will believe in you and your ability to process and make progress as you discover news ways of directing your life.

Committed & Loyal

Your helper is steadfast and faithful to you. He/She will not abandon or reject you because you do not live up to their expectations. He/She will continue to support you while challenging you to explore various ways to get the help that you need.

Has a Good Self-Image

He/She thinks positively about himself/herself and does not spend enormous amounts to time talking about self. He/She will self-disclose to you and share his/her struggles, while at the same time celebrating victories and successes achieved.

Confrontive

Your helper will not be afraid to challenge you to face your behaviors, thoughts and feelings that negatively impact your life. He or she will help you to recognize the relationship between what you say and what you do, and encourage and empower you to lovingly test your reality.

Spiritual

Your helper has a close relationship with God and encourages and challenges you to do the same.

SOME GUIDELINES FOR CHOOSING A COUNSELOR

If you are looking for a counselor here are some important things to consider.

1. He/She is reputable, and have appropriate credentials: Certified, Licensed or Registered.
2. He/She is non judgmental and respects your understanding of your problem, your beliefs, values, and philosophy of life
3. Has the personality that will make you feel comfortable.
4. Is willing to self-disclose and tell you about his/her counseling background, the clientele that he/she feels competent to help (their specialization), and why they have chosen to be a counselor. (You have the right to interview the counselor to make sure that you have enough information to make an intelligent decision.)
5. Get references from others who have been to the counselor.
6. Make sure that he/she has an unbiased theological perspective on the role and rights of women, men, headship, submission.
7. Recognizes his/her limitations, and is willing to make referrals as appropriate.
8. If you need a counselor to help you with abuse issues, be sure that he/she understands the dynamics of abuse.
9. Will respect professional/ethical boundaries:
   - Will not use you to get his/her needs met
   - Will not talk excessively about himself/herself and disregard your issues
   - Will not make inappropriate remarks about you, your body, and others.
10. He/She acknowledges your right to choose alternative solutions.

For a list of Christian counselors and therapists visit www.nadadventist.org/family and go to "resources."

FIRST REFLECTION

Negative messages are erroneous statements or ideas that people tell us by their words or actions that negatively impact what we do, say, think, and feel about ourselves and the world around us. Often these messages are given because of someone's pain, anger, bitter experiences, or ignorance. However, these messages can play in our minds day after day and can result in negative rules that we live by.

NEGATIVE MESSAGES

- ❑ Shame on you
- ❑ You're not good enough
- ❑ You won't amount to anything
- ❑ I wish you were never born
- ❑ Act like a nice girl
- ❑ Be a man
- ❑ You caused it
- ❑ You're stupid
- ❑ You owe it to us
- ❑ Be good
- ❑ You don't matter
- ❑ You make me sick
- ❑ We wanted a boy
- ❑ We wanted a girl
- ❑ You don't do things right
- ❑ You are too tall
- ❑ You are too thin
- ❑ You are too fat
- ❑ You are too short
- ❑ Why can't you be like....
- ❑ Hurry up and grow up
- ❑ I wish you were dead
- ❑ You're not intelligent enough
- ❑ I don't care what you do
- ❑ Don't be like that
- ❑ ____________________
- ❑ ____________________

NEGATIVE RULES

- ❑ Don't express your feelings
- ❑ Don't get angry
- ❑ Don't cry
- ❑ Do as I say, not as I do
- ❑ Avoid conflict
- ❑ Don't talk
- ❑ Don't think
- ❑ Always look good
- ❑ Be strong
- ❑ Maintain the family's image
- ❑ Keep family secrets
- ❑ You can't trust outsiders
- ❑ Ask no questions, just follow directions
- ❑ Don't feel
- ❑ Don't ask for help
- ❑ Don't have needs
- ❑ Be perfect
- ❑ Do not air your dirty linen
- ❑ Pretend
- ❑ Don't share
- ❑ Don't trust people
- ❑ Always be the best
- ❑ ____________________
- ❑ ____________________
- ❑ ____________________
- ❑ ____________________

As you reflect on the negative messages and rules, answer the following questions.

How did the message(s) affect me as I was growing up?

How does/do the message(s) affect me today?

How did the rule(s) affect me as I was growing up?

How does/do the rule(s) affect me today?

The plant that reminds me of myself is a

Because

I am different from everyone else because

I will celebrate my being today by

SECOND REFLECTION

Positive messages are those statements and ideas given to you by individuals that have a positive impact on your life. These statements help you feel good about yourself, increase your self-esteem and assure you that you are a valuable person. These messages help you set positive rules for your life and help you to develop satisfying and fulfilling values that empower you to be a healthy person who will form healthy relationships.

Following is a list of positive messages and positive rules for yourself and others. Read them over every day. You can add to the list. Each day claim a different message or rule and put it into practice. Next to each message and rule is a line. Use it to write the date you will practice the message and/or rule. Add your own positive messages and rules in the blank lines provided.

POSITIVE MESSAGES

___ I am wonderful
___ I know that I can do it
___ I am special
___ I can improve
___ I can make it happen
___ I did a good job
___ I belong here
___ I can try again
___ I deserve to be happy
___ I did it!
___ I enjoy being me
___ I have skills and talents
___ I have great ideas
___ I am important to God
___ I have come a long way
___ I am lovable
___ I am capable
___ I can make a difference to someone
___ I am making progress
___ I can discover new things
___ I am a winner
___ I have the right to be alive
___ I like who I am
___ ____________________
___ ____________________
___ ____________________

POSITIVE RULES

___ I can ask for help
___ I celebrate me
___ I can have time for myself
___ I can forgive and heal
___ I can test and choose friends
___ I can define my role
___ I can express my feelings
___ I can be happy
___ I can cry
___ I can grieve losses
___ I can look forward to tomorrow
___ I can set limits
___ I can explore without knowing what I am looking for
___ I can be still
___ I can forgive myself
___ I can make mistakes
___ I can be assertive
___ I can think for myself
___ I can be unique
___ I can start over
___ I can grow and change
___ I am respectable
___ ____________________
___ ____________________
___ ____________________

Remember that thinking positive thoughts about yourself is a process. Do not get discouraged if you revert back to negative thinking. If you keep talking positively to yourself, you will think positively. Keep practicing! It is not easy to move from the habit of using negative messages towards the habit of using positive ones. Doing this exercise daily is a powerful bridge towards wellness and wholeness.

If possible, try to involve all of your significant others in this exercise. This will help to make your journey of healing a pleasant and empowering experience.

Rehearse these positive messages from God:

> " ... I am with you. Do not be dismayed, for I am your God. I will strengthen you. I will help you. I will hold you up with the right hand of my righteousness" Isaiah 41:10.

> "I have loved you with an everlasting love and have been faithful to you in the past; I will continue to love you and draw you to me" Jeremiah 31:3.

> "I'll always be with you, even until the end of the world" Matthew 28:20.

> "Come to me, you who are tired and worried, and I will give you rest" Matthew 11:28.

> "I'm going home to prepare a place for you. And if I go to prepare a place for you, you can be sure that I'll come back to take you home with me, so you can be with me forever" John 14:2, 3.

NO MORE WEAPONS

Nancy's Story

As I look back to my earliest childhood memory, I see a little girl that was a very happy, actually, a spoiled child. I even know the date of my first memory. It was a day that would change my life forever. It was July 28, 1951. That morning two of my older brothers and I went across the road to watch the neighbor milk cows. I remember it vividly. I remember the milk house; the tin cup with the warm milk Mr. Moore gave me; the fact that I was bare footed and had on a cotton dress with flowers on it; my hair was very light blonde, long and hanging around my face. Why these things are so vivid, I don't know, but they are. I was just three years and two weeks old, and the apple of my family's eye.

My father had an income that was slightly above average, so we were one of the first people in our neighborhood to get a TV. One day Dad was going to put up the TV antenna before we went to the family reunion in the afternoon. My oldest brother was helping Mom with some chores, and my other two brothers took me with them to visit a neighbor.

As the three of us were on our way back from the neighbors I could feel the gravel under my feet as I walked across the road, and the sun was very bright. My brothers were one on each side of me, to keep me safe, as we crossed the road. As I looked at Dad, he was just lifting the TV antenna into the air, then he did the strangest thing. He dropped it, and then flipped to his back on the ground, then his stomach, and again to his back. I didn't understand why he would do such a strange thing, but it scared me. We ran the rest of the way across the road but my oldest brother and Mom got there first. Then a lot of people came and I got lost in the crowd. I didn't know why they took my daddy away but I never saw him again. In later years as people talked, I learned that my dad had been electrocuted when the TV antenna touched the high tension wires overhead. That is why my life changed. No one in my family believed I could remember seeing Dad die. I still don't understand why the visit to Mr. Moore is so important that it stays so clear, unless it is to point out how happy we were and how things can change so fast. I do know I missed my dad, and no one would talk to me about him because, "I was too young to be affected." WRONG! In my mind my dad had abandoned me.

We moved shortly after Dad's death. Three times! My mom took to drinking, and my brothers took to fighting. I got lost. Mom would come home from the bar, pass out on the bed with a bucket at her head and a fan at her feet, and I would stand at the end of the bed and cry, because I was afraid she was going to die too. Whenever anyone caught me crying they would laugh at me for being such a baby. I felt neglected!

I was almost five when someone knocked on our door and I answered it. Too bad I didn't pretend there was no one home. Again the picture is very clear of a little girl in shorts, straggly hair and no shoes. I still don't like to wear shoes in the house. The man at the door was tall and he was smiling and he wanted to see my mom. He came to do some work and stayed with us until he died in 1983.

He and Mom went drinking and dancing together, and he made Mom happy, so that made me happy. Actually, he was very attentive to me, too. He always told me I was his girl. He always told me my hair was pretty. He always took me with him to the store or any little place and gave me some attention of my own. I wasn't lost anymore. I had a new Daddy! It was great.

We moved again, this time out into the country. The rent didn't get paid so we had to move again, and this time we moved further out into the country and into a barn! We were very poor. We had no electricity or running water, hardly any clothes and what we did have were handed down from my stepfather's grown children.

While we lived in the barn two of my little brothers were born. Now the fighting really started. I would wake up in the night hearing him yell at my mother. I was scared! My older brothers would never talk about it, but as they turned 16 they left home one by one.

Sometimes when we would just be out for a ride, if my Mom didn't sit close enough to him in the car he would get mad. He wanted her to wear a dress all the time and he wanted her to sit in the car seat very close to him so he could play, as he put it. If she sat by her own door he would start screaming and threaten to push her out the door while we were going down the road. Of course she would move over by him and do what he wanted.

When we moved into a house the layout was not conducive to privacy of any kind. There were no bedroom doors. The nightly fights continued and got even worse. Two more babies came along and my mother was sick a lot. During this time I was not physically abused, but the ground work was all in place. Mom was so tired and so sick that a lot of responsibility fell on me: the house, the kids, her. No one had time for me; I was just a little kid myself. Ah ...but my stepfather paid attention to me. He still told me I was pretty and petted my hair. As I started to develop he held me closer and petted some more. I didn't say anything because he wouldn't do this if he didn't love me. I wanted desperately to be loved. Later I would hate the sight of him, let alone the touch of him.

One evening he and my mother went out, and I was left at home with the kids. After putting them to bed I went back to the living room to lay on the couch and watch TV. To this day, I feel pain when I see a television. As any 11-year-old kid might do I fell asleep on the couch. Finally they came home. He poured my mother into bed, (she was drunk and unconscious) and came back for me. He had touched and patted and made me feel very special (yet dirty) and now was to be the time! When I woke up he was already undressed and in the process of undressing me. I didn't like what was happening so I objected. That didn't matter, he just kept right on, and all the while he was raping me, he was telling me, "I am giving you just what I know you want."

I had never objected to the touches or to the sweet words before...it must have been my fault! I blamed myself for a long time. I told my mother. She said she didn't believe me. If I hadn't wanted it, wouldn't I have stopped it before it went so far? So it must have been my fault!

The following winter we went to Florida, in a little eight-by-eighteen trailer. Mom and her husband slept in the lower bunk and it was made clear to me I was to sleep in the front on the top bunk so my two little brothers wouldn't fall off. Every night after we were all sleeping, hands would creep up into my bed from below. He would do all sorts of evil things. I had to get away. What does an 11-year-old do? I talked to my Mom when he was away, and told her the bed was too crowded and the boys were taking their naps without falling, so they could sleep at night without falling, too. She finally agreed to let me sleep in the car, which I did for the next two-and-a-half months. There was a big fight over it but my mother didn't give in for a change. I can't help but wonder if she knew what was going on and this was her way of helping me.

He never gave up trying to get me alone. He would come into my room at night, but I had put my bed against the wall and two of the little kids could sleep with me every night. He couldn't reach me because I put them on the front of the bed.

There are so many other things, like going hungry, and the neighbors feeding us while he ate steak. But what I want to share with you at this point is that the abuse did not stop with me. I became a very protective mother...a hovering mother hen. But it was all to keep the secret - and not let it happen in my family. I vowed it would not happen in my family, NO WAY. But I didn't have good role models to follow. I never sexually abused my children, but I yelled a lot. There were times when they got spankings that could very well have turned into beatings if I hadn't been so frightened of someone finding out. I love my children and I did my best. I was so deep in denial I thought I was the best mom in the world. It still makes me sick to think how my kids suffered because of me. (My oldest daughter says, "Mom you are too hard on yourself. You did a lot more right than you did wrong.")

As I said the abuse did not stop with me. Three years ago my oldest daughter came to my husband and I and told us that she had been abused by my abuser's son when she was just seven or eight years old. Not only her but three of her cousins. And it does not stop there...it has gone into the third generation. This genealogic transfer must stop. I want to help others to know it is possible to get healing help. When we come to a group session, we come seeking answers. When we start getting those answers sometimes we don't want to come back, but the group becomes the safe place where we can be ourselves. We can take off our masks and tell the truth and know we are not alone. There are many texts in the Bible that give me comfort, but the one that helped me the most is found in Isaiah 59:19, last part:

When the enemy shall come in like a flood, the Spirit of the Lord shall lift up a standard against him.

All that I have told you was a weapon against me for years. Getting involved with recovery has become a tool to help others. That makes life worth living. I found out I'm a child of the King and if Jesus loves me enough to shed His blood for me, I am not worthless as I had thought.

THE TRUTH ABOUT YOU

by Winston Ferris

You are the direct descendent of the first members of a race:

- Created as a new and unique order of intelligent beings;
- Created in the image of God Himself;
- Created to exercise dominion and authority over Earth and its creatures;
- Created to know God and fellowship intimately with Him;
- Created to live forever in perfect health of body, mind, spirit and character;
- Created with unlimited capacity to grow;
- Created to take the place of the fallen angels as God's universal servants.

Anything in human experience that is less…
Anything in your personal experience that is less…
than any one of these in–created factors is totally the results of sin and sin's author–Satan, the former prime minister of heaven and God's sworn enemy.

Anything in you that is less…
Anything in you that is different…
Anything in you that is not full, complete and whole…
Is not *you–It is the effect of sin and its author.*

Any condition,
any belief,
any attitude,
any logic,
any conclusion
different from God's design from you *is a satanic lie.*

Only God's plan,
God's design,
God's purpose,
God's will for you is the *truth about you!*

As a Christian, this knowledge about yourself is your secret,
this is your strength,
this is your challenge,
this is your weapon,
this is your source of victory over both sin and Satan.

This knowledge is your source of power as the image of God is being restored and renewed in you by Jesus Christ.

(used by permission)

I PRAISE YOU

I praise You, Jehovah
And thank You for all You've done.
I praise Your Holy name
For battles already won.
I praise You, Redeemer
For loving me through my woes.
I sing and shout, Hallelujah
For giving me triumph over my foes.
I praise You, Lord
For giving me shelter and rest.
I praise you, Holy One
For helping bear each test.
I praise You, Jesus
For all You've given up for me.
I praise You, and thank You, Savior
For giving me life and eternity.

C H A P T E R   T W O

Our Right to Individuality

"But as many as received Him, to them gave He power to become the sons (daughters) of God" John 1:12.

Eventually I married a wonderful man. But doubts about my self-worth lingered: Why did he marry me when he could have had a more attractive and talented wife? Would he be sorry for asking me to be his wife? Would he leave me in a few years for another woman? Would he still love me when I get old, overweight, and slow? I decided that I would be the best wife, the best mother, the best Superwoman the world would ever know. I would not give anyone, including my devoted husband, any reason to abandon or reject me.

With these unrealistic goals and aspirations I became overwhelmed at trying to be the perfect human being. I was discouraged and disillusioned with life and prayed to die. "Lord, take me now, but not before You save me." In the midst of this emotional turmoil and irrational thinking, I heard a voice saying, "Mable, you have no control over where you came from, but you have control over where you are going." It was my mother's voice.

But the voice only made me get angrier. Why did she allow herself to get raped? Why didn't she do something to make my father stop his violation of her? Why didn't she get married when she was pregnant with me so that I could be "legitimate"? My life was full of misery, and it was all her fault.

I tried hard to belong. I wanted to please everyone but became frustrated because some people liked me and others didn't. Some appreciated me for working hard for the Lord, while others criticized and rejected me for being ***too*** active in the church. It seemed as if the harder I tried to be everything to everyone, the worse I felt. I reached the point in my life where I did not even know myself. I was lost. Yet to anyone observing me, I appeared happy, healthy, and holy.

HOW WE LIMIT OUR INDIVIDUALITY OR PERSONAL POWER

Personal Power: Recognition of internal, untapped, undiscovered supply of creativity, courage, potential, strength. It is not a power over others, but an innate, deep-rooted belief that I have within me the resources to direct and control my life towards self-authenticity, self-fulfillment and self-appreciation.

We create and maintain an identity which defines self as not having needs.

Through some painful experiences we learned that if we act in certain ways, others will reject us. We keep quiet instead of letting others know that they hurt us. We are compliant and accommodating instead of standing up for what we believe. We are afraid to voice our needs, because we think that we will appear to be "weak" "shallow" or "needy." We live a life full of anguish, pain, and desperation. We work so hard at maintaining this pseudo-identity that we have a hard time recognizing our true selves.

We intellectualize rather than express emotional hunger.

Rather than articulate our desires, we rationalize with ourselves and others on superficial levels. We say what we don't mean. We don't take the time to discover and understand our emotional hunger. We color our true desires with flowery words and expressions to mask feelings of inadequacy and discontent with our lives. Inwardly we want to shout out our need to be loved, touched, understood, appreciated, accepted, valued, and validated. Rather than tell the truth about our needs we lie. We begin to die!

We are afraid to show or tell who we are for fear of rejection or abandonment.

Sometimes the fear of abandonment, rejection, or loneliness rule over the truth of who we are: our needs, our dreams, our fears, our pain. We pretend to be someone else. We believe if we appear to have problems, and are honest in appraising ourselves as having weaknesses, those who are close to us might leave us. Because we did not learn how to value and appreciate who we are, we believe that other people are better than we are.

We rehearse negative messages to the extent that they keep us from exploring, changing or growing.

We continue to tell ourselves that our parents, siblings, teachers, and adults told us the truth about who we were when we were children.

We rehearse these messages over and over again until they become our "words of life." Because many of the messages tell us what we can and cannot do, who we can or cannot be, we do not question their authenticity. We journey, believing that we cannot change or grow. We avoid the challenges that beckon us to explore our individuality, relationships, and world.

We continue to practice dysfunctional and destructive behaviors.

We might try to assert ourselves in ways that will be acceptable to others. But our attempts don't seem to make much of a difference. People still treat us with indifference. We find ourselves trying to live up to their unrealistic expectations of us. Each time we do that we lose touch with who we are. We live in a maze. We become confused and frustrated. The inner turbulence becomes unbearable. Relief comes from external pain that soothes our feelings of shame and guilt. We know that we should not hurt ourselves, abuse substances, or allow our bodies to be violated. But we don't stop. Destructive behaviors are a cry for help. Because we think that we are not good enough, we don't believe that anyone cares enough to love us or help us.

We absorb the identity of our significant other/s.

"I wish you would act like…" Early in life we were probably compared to or with some one else. We were told to be good and set an example for others. When we got older and formed relationships we assumed that to please the significant people in our lives we should be like them or the kind of person they wanted us to be. At times we absorb another person's identity or some other "pleasing" personality. We talk, act, and think like someone else. We don't believe that people would like or accept who we really are. When we pretend to be someone else we are robbing the people who love us and who we love from having an honest relationship with us. We are unique and special just the way we are. As we journey through life it is a challenge to maintain and improve our own identity. But it's even harder trying to be like someone else.

We return to relationships/situations that are not good for us because we do not believe that we deserve better or can get better.

We were told that no one else wants us. That no one else will appreciate who we are. We were told that we are unattractive, stupid, and incompetent. Even though the messages come from dysfunctional people, we still believe them. Rather than live alone, we go back to relationships that make us feel bad about ourselves. We rationalize that it's better to be unhappy than alone. After all, "everybody needs somebody." When we trust God we will have the ability to choose that "somebody," and he/she will praise God for us, and we will thank God for him/her. If we cannot thank God for the relationship we should question its reliability and validity. We should be motivated to end it, or transform it so that God can bless it.

We believe that in putting others first we are humble, self-less, and ultimately a "good" Christian.

Being a good Christian does not mean that we should be someone's doormat. It does not mean that we should buckle under and conform to the dictates of others. It means that we are followers of Christ, that we will pattern His life and seek to let His radical and redemptive principles permeate our being and our actions. We love as He loves. We stand for truth. We will not allow ANYONE to have power and control over us. Following Christ is a choice not a demand. If someone is making unreasonable demands of you, demands that dishonor Christ or dishonor you, they are not being led by Christ. Therefore you cannot trust their judgment of you or your actions!

We do not challenge God because we are afraid of Him. We feel unworthy of His love. We believe the devil's lies.

The devil wants us to believe that God is a tyrant who enjoys seeing us suffer. That He waits for us to mess up, then laughs at us. Satan tries to argue with us: how could a loving God allow children to be abused? How could He allow good people to die? How could He remain silent when there are so many problems in the world: famines, diseases, earthquakes, cold-hearted people? If He truly loves people, wouldn't He intervene and stop the madness?

NEWS BULLETIN!

What the devil is not telling us is that he is the author of all the confusion and troubles we are experiencing. He is the one that wants to destroy us because God loves us. The devil uses force to get his own way, then he blames Jesus for the results. *"It is no part of Christ's mission to compel men (women) to receive Him. It is Satan, and men (women) actuated by his spirit, who seek to compel the conscience" Ellen G. White,* The Acts of Apostles, *p.541.*

Don't be fooled by Satan. Jesus has promised to deliver us. He wants to develop a relationship with us, and when we trust Him, He will show us His power and His love. He does not force us to serve Him before we prove Him. He has assured us that He will always love us, protect us, and take care of us even though we might experience some tragedy in our lives. He is always there!

> *There was an atheist couple who had a child. The couple never told their daughter anything about the Lord. One night when the little girl was five years old, the parents fought with each other, and the dad shot the mom, right in front of the child. Then, the dad shot himself. The little girl watched it all. She then was sent to a foster home. The foster mother was a Christian and took the child to church. On the first day of Sunday School, the foster mother told the teacher that the girl had never heard of Jesus, and to have patience with her. The teacher held up a picture of Jesus and said,"Does anyone know who this is?" The little girl said, "I do; that's the Man who was holding me the night my parents died"*-Author Unknown

AFFIRMATION OF OUR PERSONAL POWER

Fact:

I have the right to terminate conversations/relationships with people who make me feel put down and humiliated.

Message:

If I am in the company of an individual or individuals who make me feel ashamed, embarrassed, or put down, I will excuse myself from their presence. I will not keep a close relationship with them and give them the opportunity to berate or belittle me again. I will remember that Jesus takes the burden of my insult.

Affirmation:

"Listen to me,__________ who know what is right, you who have my law in your hearts. Don't be afraid of what people say about you. Don't be hurt by their insults" Isaiah 51:7.

"We should be encouraging one another as true brothers and sisters do, building each other up. Even Christ didn't live for Himself. As the Scriptures say, 'The insults they will hurl at you I will take on Me'" Romans 15:3.

Fact:

I have the right to experience and let go of fear, guilt, and shame.

Message:

There are times when I will be afraid. I might feel guilty and ashamed of some of the choices I make. But I don't have to let them weigh me down and keep me angry or depressed. I will ask for forgiveness when I have wronged myself, others, or God. Then I can put it behind me knowing that I am forgiven. As I continue my journey, I will remember that I cannot change the past, but I can challenge my present, and plan my future.

Affirmation:

"God does not want me to be timid and fearful, but through the Holy Spirit He has given me power, love and sound judgment. I will not be ashamed to be a disciple of Jesus Christ....God will give me the strength and fortitude I need" 2 Timothy 1:7, 8.

Fact:

I have the right to my own personal space and time needs.

Message:

I will establish a place where I can go to find safety and peace. It does not have to be elaborate or spacious. It can be small, comfortable and cosy. I can decorate and furnish it according to my taste and style. I will give myself permission to take a day, an hour, or a few minutes to visit my personal space and enjoy being with myself.

Affirmation:

"The Lord is my Shepherd, I will lack nothing. He lets me lie down in green pastures. He leads me beside quiet waters" Psalm 23:1, 2.

"When every other voice is hushed, when every earthly interest is turned aside, the silence of the soul makes more distinct the voice of God. Here rest is found in Him. The peace, the joy, the life of the soul, is God" Ellen G. White, *Fundamentals in Christian Education*, p. 440.

Fact

I have the right to my own identity.

Message:

"You are you. God made you, you. And you are exactly who He wants you to be. Don't be somebody's clone. That person you're trying to be may very well be trying to be you." Luci Swindoll

Affirmation:

"God requires that the wife (woman) shall keep the fear and the glory of God ever before her. Entire submission is to be made only to the Lord Jesus Christ, who has purchased her as His own child by the infinite price of His life. God has given her a conscience which she cannot violate with impunity. Her individuality cannot be merged into that of her husband (significant other) for she is the purchase of Christ" Ellen G. White, *Letter 18*, 1891.

Fact:

I have the right to change, expand, and grow.

Message:

I will change some of my thoughts and behaviors that have not been productive in my life. As I change I will add new dimensions to my thoughts and actions. I will read, write, create, and grow. Even though growth can be painful, it is rewarding. I suffered pain because of what others did to me, or said about me, or failed to give me. But now, the pain will be different. It will be the kind of pain that a butterfly endures when it must break out of its cocoon and transform into a beautiful creature. Butterflies have wings. Like a butterfly, I will fly when I am ready.

Affirmation:

"He gives strength to those who are weak and energy to those who are weary. Even young men become weak and stumble and fall. But those who wait on the Lord and go to Him for help will have their strength renewed. They will soar like eagles" Isaiah 40: 29-31.

A man found a cocoon of a butterfly. One day a small opening appeared. He sat and watched the butterfly for several hours as it struggled to force its body through that little hole. Then it seemed to stop making any progress. It appeared as if it had gotten as far as it could and it could go no further. So the man decided to help the butterfly. He took a pair of scissors and snipped off the remaining bit of the cocoon. The butterfly then emerged easily. But it had a swollen body and small, shriveled wings. The man continued to watch the butterfly because he expected that, at any moment, the wings would enlarge and expand to be able to support the body, which would contract in time. Neither happened! In fact, the butterfly spent the rest of its life crawling around with a swollen body and shriveled wings. It never was able to fly. What the man in his kindness and haste did not understand was that the restricting cocoon and the struggle required for the butterfly to get through the tiny opening were God's way of forcing fluid from the body of the butterfly into its wings so that it would be ready for flight once it achieved its freedom from the cocoon.

Sometimes struggles are exactly what we need in our life. If God allowed us to go through our life without any obstacles, it would cripple us. We would not be as strong as what we could have been. We could never fly. Author Unknown.

Fact:

I have the right to forgive others and forgive myself.

Message:

It is difficult to think of forgiving those who abused me, neglected me, violated my universal rights, and misjudged me. But I will choose to let go of my anger towards them and recognize that they must deal with the evil deeds they did to me. I will not let my mind become dulled and dwarfed by dwelling upon revengeful thoughts towards them. Doing so robs me of precious energy that I need in order to recover from their abuse. When possible and/or appropriate I will let them know that they hurt me and contributed to my feelings of inadequacy and low self-worth. I will hold them accountable for their actions. I will not blame myself and feel guilty for my past experiences. Some of the experiences I could not have avoided. There were probably others that I could have avoided but did not. But today I will move on. I will acknowledge that some of the things I did was to fill a need. I will continue to explore positive ways to fulfill my needs so that I will no longer be a victim. I will be victorious. There is a time for everything. Now is my time to move on.

Affirmation:

"There are other things I've learned about life.
There are times to do specific things and different seasons in which to do them.
There is a certain day when you're born and then comes a certain day when you die.
There is a time to plant and a time to harvest what was planted.
There are times when we must let things die, and there are also times to bring about healing.
There are times to tear things down and times to build again.
There are times in life when we need to weep and other times when we need to laugh.
There are times of sorrow and times of joy.
There are times to love and times not to love.
There are times to hug and times not to hug.
There are times when we find things and times when we lose things.
There are times to keep things and times to throw them away.
There are times when we must part and times when we come together again.
There are times to speak and times to keep silent.

There are times to express love and times to express disapproval. There are times to go to war and times to make peace.

...In the beginning He made everything beautiful and created* _______________in His own image. He put in _____________'s heart a sense of time and eternity, but_____________ will never understand everything that God plans and does. Whatever happens to________ in her/his lifetime has happened before. And God takes the past, present and future into account when He makes His decisions" -Ecclesiastes 3:1-8, 11, 15.

*Insert your name in the blank lines.

Fact:

I have the right to love and be loved.

Message:

I can choose to love others. It does not mean that they will love me in return. When I am free to love, I am releasing myself to be me. I will share myself and open myself to that love when I know that it is safe and comfortable to do so. I will do the best I can to be kind and gentle to myself. I will go easy on myself and treat myself as someone I really love. When I learn to truly love myself, I will allow others to love me, for I am loveable.

Affirmation:

"We know and believe that God loves us, and anyone who lives a loving life is living in harmony with God. Fear and love just don't go together. Love dispels fear because fear focuses on punishment and won't let us grow as we should. The one who is afraid of God has not understood the depth of God's love. We love God because He first loved us. That's where our love comes from" I John 16, 18, 19.

Fact:

I have the right to try out different roles and ways of being powerful.

Message:

I acknowledge that I can do many things. Because of the various responsibilities I have I wear different hats; I play different roles. I am realizing that this means I have talent, I am adaptable. I am a creative and versatile person. Sometimes I find myself doing five things at a time: washing clothes, cooking, answering the telephone, ironing clothes, and working on a project. Now that I am taking out time to reflect on all that I do, I realize that I have personal power. This power comes from the Lord. I must preserve who I am, because in all the world, no two people are exactly alike. And even though other people might be able to do what I do, I am the only one that will do it the way I do it. That makes me unique. What I do does not define me but I define what I do.

Affirmation:

"I can face any situation with Christ who gives me strength." Philippians 4:13.

Exercise #1 - Who Am I?

Take out time to reflect on the following statements and write your answers in the space provided. You can do this when you are in your personal space.

My specific needs at this time are ______________________________

____

____

____

I am the kind of person who enjoys______________________________

____

____

____

I feel rejected by others when they______________________________

____

____

____

Some destructive behaviors I continue to practice are_______________

____

____

____

I believe that if someone really loves me they will not ______________

____

____

____

I would like to be the kind of person who_________________________

____

____

____

Some of the steps that I can take to be that person include:

i.____

____

____

____

ii. ______________________________

iii. ______________________________

iv. ______________________________

v. ______________________________

My Power Defined

(A Paraphrase of I Corinthians 13)

Even though I can speak eloquently and influence a large audience to respond to the love of God, if I do not have His love in my heart, I am only full of noise. And if people are drawn to me because of my charming and winsome personality, they will soon turn their backs on God.

Even if I have the ability to predict things, am very intuitive; able to understand those things that seem mysterious; have several degrees and expertise in many areas; and believe that I can accomplish anything I put my mind to, like moving a mountain, without love, my accomplishments are worthless.

Even though I give all of my money, clothes, and food to the poor and needy and sacrifice myself by working hard in the church, giving Bible studies, and attending every service, and go through fire, floods, hurricanes, earthquakes, if I don't love, my motives are wrong, and I am nothing.

My love for others should not end because they get sick, grow old, lose a job, or don't live up to my expectations. True love is kind. It is not jealous and possessive. It does not seek to have power and control over another. Rather, it encourage me to love others as Christ loves me, and give of myself to help others as He gives of Himself to me.

Love does not do that which is improper, making me feel ashamed, guilty or uncomfortable. Love is not self-centered. It is not rude or disrespectful. It will encourage me to respect the dignity and integrity of others. It will not dwell on other's mistakes and keep a journal of their failures. Love will not be accusing. It will motivate me to think the best of others. It will act in ways that will allow me to use my potential for God's glory, while I allow others to do the same.

Love will not perpetuate evil. It will not cause me to look at evil, talk of evil, or practice evil. It will speak the truth. Love will not knowingly allow me to cause anyone else pain. For a disposition to cause pain comes from the devil. Love will not permit me to keep secrets that are detrimental to others. It will hold me accountable for my actions, while inviting others to find grace through Jesus Christ.

Love will forbear under all circumstances. It will help me to believe that I can change, and people can change. It will hope for the best and it will stand the test of time. It will give me and others the opportunity to live in safe environments.

Love will not fail in times of poverty or discouragement. Love will not allow me to disregard others or talk badly of them. One day my predictions will cease. One day my ability to speak in many languages will end. Many things that I am learning now will not be of any value, for they will pass away.

Even the vast knowledge that I might have regarding technology and science will end. What I can predict only gives me a cloudy and limited vision of the future.

When time is ended, more of God's knowledge will be imparted to me. I will totally understand why I had to go through experiences that caused me grief and pain. But whatever I do not fully understand before this will not matter, because He will take away my sorrow. He will wipe away my tears when He comes, because pain will be gone forever.

When I was young, I spoke like children do. My understanding was very childish. As I grew up I realized that my immature thinking and actions were keeping me from becoming an adult. Some of them I put away. Some I did not.

Today, some things are still not clear to me. I don't understand why I suffer so much, why life is so hard. I don't understand why I carry so much anger, bitterness, resentment, guilt and shame. I don't understand why people are victimized or perpetuate crime. But love motivates me to get help if I am in need of recovery, so that I can truly support others. I must do the best I can to foster a non- violent relationship and rest assured that when Jesus comes, He will answer all of my questions. For it is only then that I will truly understand. For now, He only reveals to me what He wants me to know. Until then, I need to be patient and trust Him to take care of me whether I have family, friends or am alone.

There are three very important gifts that God has given me: Faith in Him, hope for the future, and unconditional love. But the greatest gift of all is unconditional love not only for others, but also for myself.

"People will know that you are my disciples by how much you love each other" John 13:35.

Love defines you as a powerful person!

Exercise #2 - Defining Self By Love

What does unconditional love mean to you?

Do you love yourself unconditionally?

If not, why not?

Do you love others unconditionally?

If not, why not?

How can you celebrate your personal power?

What are some ways in which you are powerful now?

Other ways in which you will be powerful:

A.

B.

C.

THE FUTURE IS MINE

Dawn's Story

I met my husband in the summer. He was charming, polite, a hard worker, but best of all he was a Christian. On our first date he reached across the table in a public restaurant, held my hand, and prayed out loud. He attended church with me. I have children from a former marriage. He played ball with the boys and bought the children gifts. He had always wanted a "large family." As winter approached he took off time from his job to cheer my boys on at their Christian school basketball games. He read stories to my little girl. Always the gentleman, he sent flowers to my office, left special cards in my home where I would find them later. He did not pressure me for intimacy.

We went out on several dates before he asked my permission to kiss me good night. My friends and family thought he was wonderful for me and my children. At the first of the year he took me to a well-known restaurant and sang his proposal to me. Among the cheering patrons, I agreed to be his wife. The restaurant made a tape of the song and proposal which we played for the children the next day. They were reserved in their responses, but in my happiness I attributed their hesitancy to the normal confusion of mixing families.

Once we were engaged, certain changes occurred that, in retrospect, were predictors of our future life together. My husband felt that it was very important that he establish the idea in my children that once we were married they were to submit to him as head of the household and that he had certain rules and expectations they would be expected to honor. The "rules" that he outlined were not unreasonable. The children were to take turns with the household chores. They were not to talk back to me and were to be respectful of him. They would be responsible for cleaning their rooms. I had retained full custody of my children and for seven years had been raising them alone. The children were already responsible for many tasks and chores. It was important that we maintained a regular schedule of morning showers, meals, school, music, homework, sports, etc. A single mom learns to be organized as she and her children endeavor to get all their needs met.

My husband-to-be would call "family meetings" and reiterate his concerns about our lives together. As the time approached for our wedding these family meetings became more frequent. The kids would roll their eyes, as if to say, "We've heard all of this before." I attributed these lectures to premarital nerves. Slowly my children started to back away from the relationship. Foolishly I made excuses for their reactions. I talked with my children's teachers and was told that they seemed to be having a natural reaction to change. That change is scary. Now I realized that respect has to be something earned not demanded.

My husband and I decided to forego the expense of a large wedding and were married by a Justice of the Peace. A gross misnomer in this case, because all "peace" was shattered with the pledging of "I do." In my case the definition that my husband held for "wife" was much different from the definition of "single."

On our honeymoon trip, my husband directed me to go sit in a coffee shop while he registered for a "single bed." When he collected me from the shop, the manager of the motel came to the car, knocked on the window, and informed my husband that he did not appreciate him cheating the motel and that if he didn't pay for me we would be evicted. He informed the manager that I was someone that he had just picked up and he would not be keeping me for the whole night. We then left the parking lot and drove to a grocery store to get dinner. On the way back to the motel, I had to lie on the floor so the manager would not see me. My husband went out first, motioned to me when the coast was clear, and I tried to sneak up to the room. Looking back, the manager stood watching. Of course it was all my fault that I had been seen.

After pacing the floor, swearing and cursing (I had never heard him use any profanity while we dated), he asked me what I wanted to do. I told him that I would go pay the $6 difference. He exploded. He threw me down on the bed. Jumped on top of me, choked my neck and shook me violently. Screaming "You've made me look like a fool", he threw my clothes at the suitcase, told me to get out (we were two states away from home), went down to the car and drove away. I was in shock. I did not know anyone there. I had no money. I had all my things gathered and was trying to decide whether to spend the night alone and then call someone to wire me some money or leave, when he returned. He saw my bag packed, my purse on top, and exploded again. He said that if I ever left him he would kill me. I had never experienced anything like that. I was afraid. We did not touch that night. I did not sleep.

The next day he stopped at the river boat and gambled much more than the $6. He bought me a rose and an expensive meal. He held my hand and prayed over the meal. He prayed for a long fruitful marriage. He laughed and joked. His life was normal again. Something inside of me had died. This was to be the pattern that repeated itself over and over in our marriage. Abuse, retribution, slow loss of identity.

Rules became a way of life. The problem was...the rules always changed. The children would receive hour long lectures for putting a foot on the coffee table or failure to cut spaghetti or not paying attention when he was speaking. The threats and lectures were demeaning. It would be okay to turn on a light one day, but the next day is was a violation of a rule to do the same thing. We all walked on eggshells. The father of the children asked for and was granted temporary custody alleging abuse from my husband and failure on my part to protect them. Of course, in my husband's eyes, that was the fault of the children and my ex-husband, not himself. Why didn't I leave? I do not know. Fear, perhaps. Shame? I didn't know where to go or what to do. I just existed.

Once the children were gone, he turned his system of rules toward me. I could only shower with him. I could not wash my hair without his permission (he once caught me washing my hair "behind his back" and knocked me down). I was banged against the kitchen cabinets until my shoulder blades were bloody because I dared to wear a sleeveless blouse outside to mow the lawn. "Married women do not wear sleeveless blouses." If I dared to step on the carpet with my shoes on, or tuck my foot under me on the sofa, or turn on a light after dark I was attacked. I had broken his rules. My banking accounts were closed because married couples do not need separate accounts. I was not given the account number or checks. I was given a few dollars for gas every other day. It was just enough to get me to work and back. All mail was sent to a post office box for which I did not have a key. All important papers (my children's included) and my jewelry were placed in a safe that I did not have the combination to. My husband demanded that I quit my job at a prominent university. I did not.

He would call several times a day. He would accuse me of affairs. He would sneak out of his office to check up on me. I was required to call every day before I left for home. I prayed that no one would stop me on the way out of my office and detain me with a question. If I was more that a few minutes late the accusations would begin. He demanded, and I complied, that I sign over my entire check to him. He stated that biblically it was his right as head of the household to pay the bills and control the money. All of my undergarments from my "single life" were discarded. All sleeveless, v-neck, lacy, and knee-length garments were disallowed. Every outfit was given thorough scrutiny. I was not allowed to wear any tucked in blouses. "If a man wants to look at you, he better be paying for it," he would say.

Nail polish, hair spray, curling irons, hair dryers were taboo. I was prohibited from talking to past friends and family. According to my husband, I was to forsake all others to be true to only him. We moved to another home and I was not allowed to give the address to anyone (not even my children). In a ten month span I only saw them two times. He was not going to spend the gas money to get them after what they had done to him. Stamped postcards were only 20¢. I used my coffee change to buy postcards to send my children little notes. I was not allowed to buy them birthday gifts. I was given $5 to buy Christmas presents for them. I bought them each socks. I lived in a fog of fear, shame, and confusion.

I cannot count the times in the year before I left, that I was knocked down, choked, threatened, called horrible degrading names. And again, I cannot count the times I was told that I was loved. As the cycle of attacks became more vicious the avowals of love became more adamant. His testimonial of love included telling me in detail all of the things he had done for me. He had arranged my hair appointments, he had given me gas money, he had payed the bills, he had sent me flowers. He surely must love me if he did these things. There was not one aspect of my life that was not under the control of my husband.

I longed for the man that I had fallen in love with, dated, and married. I did not want to believe that it was this man. I prayed for help. I prayed for him. I prayed for my children. I cried for the lost me. For I had lost my identity. I was no longer the mother of my children. I no longer was free to help a friend in need. I no longer was the daughter that had always been there when my mother needed me. I no longer was what God had designed. I had become an image of my husband. A reflection of his rules. What great hold had this man exerted over me that could reduce me to this state in such a short time? I still wrestle with this question.

Several times I packed a small bag to leave. I determined that there would not be a next time. I determined that I would not let him hit me ever again. A couple months after we married I found checks with the name of another woman and him embossed. When I asked about them, I found that he had been married to her two years previously and that she had left him after only six months. Subsequently, I found out that this man, my husband, had been married two times and had three fiancees in the five year span before we met. Three women filed abuse charges against him and he did community service for one of them. I do not know how many times my husband has been married. I know of four marriages. He lied on the marriage license. He has a record of violent behavior against women that dates back to his early twenties. We are now in our forties. This knowledge increased my fear. Although it is of some comfort to know that I was not the only woman taken in by his charming premarital behavior, I am still left with incredible hurt. My critical nature seems all the more cruel when directed within. I am left doubting the very attributes I once labeled as assets. I vow to not become hard or skeptical of others. I can no more live that way, now, than I did before.

I was a good mother with beautiful children, a professional woman with a BA degree and I had lovely home. I did not leave my husband until the fear of staying became greater than the fear of leaving. He told me repeatedly that if I left him, he would track me down and kill me. Twice the message had been reinforced by him getting the gun out of the cabinet and waving it at me. According to my husband, I had sworn to God that I would be true to him, as he says, "To obey until death do us part."

As a Christian, the nagging guilty message struck a cord deep within. It was my dream that had been shattered. I asked "God, where are You in all of this?" I was ashamed to tell my friends and family that I had been so wrong in my choice. My silence alienated that very source of support that could have sustained me. How foolish I had been to think that God had not heard my cries. When I finally told of my pain, my experiences, my situations, it seemed that an army of support was waiting to help me. Police assisted me in leaving my home. I could not return to my job, but my boss was very supportive and I have wonderful references for the future. I walked away with a suitcase, a few heirlooms, AND MY LIFE.

As the plight of domestic abuse has become more public, communities and churches are responding to the need. I was housed, fed, clothed, and counseled by loving, caring women that have been in my shoes. Many abused women and children have come and gone from the shelter in the month that I remained there. Across all economic, age, religion, or race differences the stories and patterns of abuse echo each other. I see women scared and lonely. Children confused...acting out scenes of violence in their play. By that design do I carry a similar fate? The sky is not less blue nor the snow yellowed for my pain. Time marches on heedless. Are these to be new eyes given by God or old ones more wizened? I get stronger day by day. The road is not easy. I still long for the dream man of my marriage. I pray for my mate that he will cry out to the God that he used so conveniently to inflict his own will on others. I realize now that I cannot change this man. Women of abuse are survivors. I have survived. Now I thrive. For a while a man took away my present. But now another Man has given me the power to take back my future.

THE TRUTH ABOUT YOUR PERSONAL POWER

You are only a jar of clay, filled with the treasures of the gospel.

To show that your power is from God and not from you.

Everywhere you go you might have trouble, but don't be discouraged.

You might be perplexed, but don't give up.

You might be persecuted, but you are never abandoned.

You might be struck down, but you are not defeated.

Because of Him, never give up, even though physically you're wearing out.

Yet every day new life and determination will spring up inside of you.

The few troubles you're having at this moment are not to be compared with the far more important glorious future.

You're not looking at things you can see, but at things unseen by humans.

What you see around you is temporary, and will soon be destroyed.

But that which can't be seen now will last forever.

2 Corinthians 4:7-9, 16-18.

BE YOU

Sometimes a quiet tear without consent
Drips from a reservoir of hurt and pain
Seeping through barricades pride cannot prevent
When human limitations feel the strain.

Don't mold yourself within another's shoe.
You travel paths they have not tread.
Don't harbor needless shame imposed on you.
Insist on being triumphant instead.

You are unique. Choose to remain that way.
With inner eyes search deep into your soul.
Internal strength will lead you day by day.
With steadfast courage you'll reach your goals.

-Ellen (my mother)

CHAPTER THREE

The Right to Think and Feel

"I think, therefore I am" Descartes

"For as he [she] thinketh in his [her] heart so is he [she]" Proverbs 23:7.

"If you allow another to do your thinking for you, you will have crippled energies and contracted abilities" Ellen G. White, Review and Herald, April 16, 1889.

"Our feelings express the way we think of ourselves, and how we react to what is going on around us. Feelings help us make distinctions between what we prefer, and what we don't prefer, what is safe and what is not safe, what is good and what is bad. If we have no feelings (numbness) we often do not know what we prefer or what is safe. If we do not have preferences, do we know who we are? If we do not know what is safe, can we protect ourselves or our children?" Mable

As time progressed I had some long talks with my mother and have asked her to forgive me for being such a rebellious and ungrateful teenager and young adult. While basking in self-pity, I did not realize how traumatic my birth had been for her. How ashamed she must have felt. I did not see how my mother had to change her goals, even her life, because she had been violated and had to deal with much pain, suffering, feelings of guilt and shame. For the first time in my life it dawned upon me that my mother was not to be blamed for what happened to her, or for what happens to me as an adult.

My experience with the boy in the back of his friend's house gave me a glimpse of the horror my mother must have encountered. I believe for those moments her experience was vividly portrayed in my mind, and I was given the chance to escape a terrible fate, something my mother never could have.

Today, I am a mother of three, and I realize that it takes great care, love, patience, and unselfish devotion to raise a child. As I thought of the way my mother took care of me, I realized that she did the best she could to nurture me so that I could experience healthy self-worth. As my feelings of anger and self-pity lessened, I have been able to love and appreciate my mother for giving me the most wonderful gift of all: LIFE. She didn't have to, but she did. Today she is my closest and dearest friend. After all we are only 18 years apart! And I praise God that she raised me in a Christian home. Not a perfect home, but a home where the desire was sown early in my heart to seek a relationship with God.

While completing my Master's degree I came across a statement that transformed my life. "Every human being created in the image of God is endowed with a power akin to that of the Creator–individuality, power to think and to do." This statement struck me because no longer did I have an excuse to blame my mother, the insensitive Christian women, my birth father, or feel sorry for myself.

God allowed me to be born! He created me in His image! He gave me power to be alive, to think, to feel, to be uniquely me, and to do! What a revelation! My mother's voice rang in my head again, "You have no control over where you came from, but you have control over where you are going."

I know that life is a gift, and I cherish that gift. It is up to me to decide what I will do with that gift regardless of what people say about me or do to me.

HOW WE LIMIT OUR THINKING AND FEELING

We may attempt to control space and people around us by being opinionated and intimidating.

We do not want people to get close to us (Yes we do). So we ward them off by holding on to our opinions. We make it difficult for them to challenge us or disagree with us. This negative behavior is our attempt to hide our emotional pain. What we really want is for them to invest the time and energy to get to know us better so that they can appreciate and accept us. We say one thing when we are feeling another.

We may act compliant so as not to think for ourselves or express our feelings and give up control of self to avoid having or maintaining a position or opinion.

Sometimes it's easier to just give in and not express our thoughts and feelings. We learned that we can avoid conflict if we keep quiet or agree with a person of power. Doing this gives them or our significant other more power and control over us. We must learn to think for ourselves and have opinions. We should be more assertive, for when we are not, we feel weak, and we betray ourselves.

We may be afraid of rejection so we do not voice an opinion.

We think of the past and remember times when we were told that we were stupid because we expressed an opinion. We might have felt isolated from family members or friends. So when we find ourselves in a situation where our differing opinion might cause others to reject us, we say nothing.

We may be afraid to explore our thoughts and feelings because we might have to change our way of life.

Change can be difficult. Even though we attend workshops and seminars, hear speeches that challenge us to change our way of life, we are afraid to do so. We hold on to the old patterns of thinking and feeling, not because they work for us, but because they are predictable.

We may be afraid to experience feelings so that we can avoid painful memories.

Sometimes we do not allow ourselves to feel. Feeling implies that we must mentally rehearse painful experiences; we might remember things that we want to forget. As we think and feel we might have to acknowledge that our parents were dysfunctional, that they probably did not love us the way they should have or the way we thought they did. We might remember that we made some mistakes; we might condemn ourselves because of the terrible things we allowed others to do to us.

We become numb, and in doing so we avoid change and growth.

If we cannot think or feel, we don't change or grow. We become numb. But this does not prevent pain. A lack of thinking and feeling develops a void within us that can give others the opportunity to use and abuse us. As we think we grow, and as we grow we can challenge how we are treated and we learn to avoid the toxic nature of others so that they do not pollute or poison us.

We hold on to past hurts which prevent us from testing and trusting new experiences and people.

Sometimes we think about how people hurt us and we hide in a tightly-wrapped protective cloak of mistrust and fear that no one can penetrate. We do not share our thoughts or feelings with them. Sometimes we miss the opportunity to form new friendships and relationships and do not get the opportunity to replace old, destructive experiences with new, productive ones.

AFFIRMATION OF OUR THOUGHTS AND FEELINGS

Fact:

I have the right to hold and express my own opinions.

Handwrite the message and affirmation. Place it on your mirror, refrigerator or somewhere you will see it regularly.

Message:

When I think and feel, I am alive and growing, not merely surviving. My thoughts and feelings tell people who I am. It tells them that I am someone to be reasoned with, someone to acknowledge, respect and appreciate.

Affirmation:

"Now these are the things I want you to do: Be honest with each other and administer true justice in your courts, the kind of justice that brings peace" Zechariah 8:16.

Fact:

I have the right to be angry at someone I love.

Message:

If someone I love makes me angry, I can let them know and not feel guilty or afraid that they will hurt me. If I think that it is not safe to be angry with them, I will find a safe place and way to release that anger. If I do not express my anger, I can explode and hurt others or implode and hurt myself.

A safe way in which I can release my anger is ____________________

____

____

A safe person with whom I can express my anger is ______________

Affirmation:

"If you get upset, don't focus on your feelings until you become hateful and degenerate into sin. Be angry with sin, but don't sin by being angry with the sinner. Determine to get over any anger before nightfall, or the devil will gain a foothold" Ephesians 4:26, 27.

Fact:

I have the right to feel and control my negative emotions.

Message:

Sometimes I feel sad, revengeful, or fearful, but I don't know the origin of these emotions. I get overwhelmed with feelings of guilt and shame. I can feel these negative emotions and explore their origin. Sometimes I will be able to determine their origin, other times I will not. I will realize they are indicators of past experiences that are affecting me. If I can identify their source I will either get rid of them or control them. As I am able to control them, I will learn how to control my life.

Affirmation:

"...He knows where I am, and when He has finished testing me, my integrity will come out as gold" Job. 23:10.

Fact:

I have the right to change my mind and feelings.

Message:

There are many things I think about. Sometimes I think that I should do something one way, then another way. As I learn, grow, study, and open up myself to new experiences, what I thought was, might not really be. If a habit or behavior is not producing the results I need or want, I can change. I don't have to feel locked into one way of feeling or thinking.

Affirmation:

"Don't be conformed to the patterns of this world, but continually renew your mind by focusing on the Lord Jesus Christ, letting Him transform you from the inside out. Then show by the way you live that God's will for you is good, acceptable and just" Romans 12:2.

Fact:

I have the right to grieve over what I didn't get that I needed, or what I got that I didn't need or want.

Message:

To grieve is to lament or regret. It is okay for me to feel deep regret over what has happened to me in the past. It Is okay for me to be sorry that certain things did not go the way I would have liked them to. There were things that I wanted that I did not or could not get: healthy parents, a beautiful home, a husband, a good marriage, children, the dream vacation, job, etc. Worrying about the past will not change it. If I find that I am grieving over my present situation, I can do something about it. I can make plans for the future. I need to remember that I had no control over what took place during my childhood, but I have control over my present and future.

Affirmation:

"Thank you, Lord, for helping me. Once again, my confidence in You is steadfast. Again, my faith is fixed. I will sing praises to You and give You thanks" Psalm 57:7.

"I will leave all of my anxieties and worries with You because You care for me" 1 Peter 5:7.

"God may not always stop others from hurting you, but it is better to suffer for doing good than for doing evil" I Peter 3:17.

"'Whenever I am worried or anxious You are the One who makes me glad and give me joy" Psalm 93:19.

Fact:

I do not have to be responsible for others' feelings or behavior.

Message:

I will probably have individuals cross my path as I journey who will want to manipulate me and make me responsible for how they are feeling. They might do this by coercing me into changing my thinking and feeling in order to accommodate their needs. I will remind them that it is their responsibility to own their thoughts and feelings, as it is my responsibility to own mine.

Affirmation:

"Each one has to give account of himself to God" Romans 14:12.

Fact:

I have the right to cry.

Message:

Crying is a constructive way to release anger, frustration, disappointment, pain, and sorrow. It can be comforting in times of depression and discouragement. In the past I might have received the message that it was childish to cry. But it is not childish to cry. It is okay for me to express my emotions in this healthy way.

Affirmation:

"Sorrow surrounded me and pain engulfed me. I felt as if I were dying. Everywhere I looked I saw trouble and sorrow. Then I called on the Lord and said, 'I beg You, O Lord, please save me!' He heard me and saved me. The Lord is merciful and gracious. He is full of compassion" Psalm 116:3-5.

"I cried to God for help. I cried out loud and He heard me. In times of trouble I sought the Lord. All night long I held up my hands in prayer but found no comfort. When I thought of you, O God, I heaved a sigh of weariness. Even after I mediated and prayed, I only felt depressed. I could not sleep. I was so troubled that I didn't even feel like talking (to You)...So I decided to think instead about the times when You were near and about the great things You have done for us. I'll think about the power of Your word, Lord, and the works of Your hands. I'll recall all the wonders You have done in the past" Psalm 77:1-4, 11-12.

Exercise #1 - Exploring Thoughts and Feelings

DIRECTIONS: On the blank line, write one word to describe how you feel as you think about each word/phrase. There are some feeling words on the opposite page that may help you.

WORD/PHRASE	FEELING
1. Motherhood	______
2. Friends	______
3. Body shape	______
4. Working outside of the home	______
5. Not going to church	______
6. Getting a degree	______
7. Housework	______
8. Sex	______
9. Career	______
10. Significant other	______
11. Children	______
12. Mission/individual ministry	______
13. Mother	______
14. Father	______
15. Brother	______
16. Sister	______
17. My hair	______
18. My height	______
19. Being a church officer/leader	______
20. Cooking	______
21. Menopause	______
22. Childbirth	______
23. Having Fun	______
24. Sleep	______
25. Vacation	______
26. Journaling	______
27. Bedroom	______
28. Other Women	______
29. Myself	______
30. Being a Woman	______

Here are some feeling words to help you.

Enthusiastic	Lazy	Rejected	Passionate
Agonized	Irritated	Enraged	Hopeful
Successful	Joyful	Arrogant	Loved
Stubborn	Discouraged	Withdrawn	Relieved
Apologetic	Shocked	Resentful	Indifferent
Determined	Ashamed	Lonely	Guilty
Exhausted	Aggravated	Hateful	Hysterical
Disgusted	Surprised	Worried	Sorry
Depressed	Pressured	Sad	Embarrassed
Proud	Jealous	Confident	Frightened
Shy	Happy	Dismayed	Hurt
Helpless	Aggressive	Nervous	Anxious
Heart-broken	Bored	Kind	Envious

Did you find it difficult to describe a feeling for any of the words or phrases?__________If yes, why?______________________________

Define the word "feeling" in your own words. ____________________

Define the word "thinking" in your own words. ____________________

What message do you receive about yourself when you begin to feel emotions of guilt, fear, shame or anger?____________________

If your message is a negative one, rewrite it so that it can be positive.

(Here's an example for you from my experience).

The negative message: "*I should have known better than to go with that boy.*"

The positive message: "*I am glad that I was able to leave an unsafe situation.*"

What thoughts are you telling yourself about your right to have and express your opinions?____________________

If your thoughts are negative, rewrite them so that they can be positive.

(Here's an example for you from my experience).

The negative message: "*No matter how hard I try, I will never be good enough.*"

The positive message: "*God's strength is made perfect in my weakness*" *2 Corinthians 2:9.*

Exercise #2 - The Picture Story

Following is the story of the picture chart. The writer is a 21-year old, and her story is true. Identifying factors have been left out of her story to protect her and her family.

Charting My Journey

In the boxes on the next page tell your journey in pictures or words before your memories of abuse, your memories after abuse, and your dream for the future.

Using the picture chart, write your story in a safe place and if necessary with safe people. As you write, allow yourself to think and feel. You have permission to feel your emotions and release them so that they will no longer have power over you. Ask God for His love, healing, and power.

BEFORE:

Before my memories of abuse I was happy. I lived with my parents. I remember feeling loved by them. But as I got older and formed relationships, I knew that something was terribly wrong. Someone molested me in my home and I began to show my anger and do things that caused my parents to put me out of their home. I became pregnant. My parents were "good Christians." They felt embarrassed that their daughter had an illegitimate child. So I had to leave home.

AFTER:

I lived in an apartment that was not very safe. Soon I got involved with friends who enticed me to do some things that were not very good. The father of my child ended up in jail. I don't know why I didn't go to jail too. It's only now I believe that God was with me. I was raped several times. I got pregnant again. I began drinking, smoking and taking drugs. I almost died. Some of my friends died.

MY DREAM:

I want to get married and live a good life. I want to see my children saved. I want my entire family to be saved.

(If you continue to struggle with negative, destructive thoughts and feelings that threaten your well-being or the well-being of others, you should get professional help).

BEFORE	AFTER	DREAM
1	1	1
2	2	2
3	3	3

"THE SUNSHINE KID"

Mark's Story

My abuse came when I left Grassland Hospital in Val Halla, New York. I went into the hospital at age four and let out at five-and-a-half years old. I was moved from Grassland to the children's hospital called Sunshine Cottage also in Val Halla. I went in with Cerebral Spinal Meningitis and complications of Tuberculosis.

I started 1st grade late. I was a slow learner, sickly, tired a lot, but was told (by others) that I had a heart of gold. My reading habits were poor also. My first grade teacher, Mrs. Smith, was very kind to me. There were times when I fell asleep in class due to Mom and Dad fighting, and crying during the nights, not feeling good, or just the pressure of coming back to the Projects after school to deal with Mom, saying "You look and act just like your father. You are dumb, slow, have large ears, and nobody has a large nose in this family but you."

Mrs. Smith's class was where kind, and positive things were said to me. She told me I was important and that maybe I would be a doctor or work in the medical field to help other people (children) find a cure for the Meningitis that made me ill. Mrs. Smith always gave me warm, strong hugs, even when I had detention (I am crying now as I write my story. This is painful). When it came to reading, my mother would hit my hands or knuckles with a large soup spoon or fork. I was in this relationship because I had no where else to go. She would hit my hands because I didn't pronounce words right or I read too slow. By the time I was in fifth grade, she had pulled my ears so hard that I have a hearing problem today. I also failed my physical for the Army in

1968 for Vietnam War. It would leave me dizzy. I've been slapped in the face, nose and mouth. Mom has beaten me to the floor, kicked me in my behind, stomach and spine. I've been hit with a shoe, thick belt, broom, paddle, even an extension cord which left welts in my arms, back, and legs for weeks. The school nurse made records of this and the principal saw it.

In a few rare outbursts, Mom would spit on me. I remember when the nurse saw my back, and got the principal. They asked me what bully did this to me. I couldn't talk. They got so upset with me that they said they would call my Mother at work to let her know that a bully in the Projects had done this to me.

By that time I broke down and cried. The nurse and principal looked at each other questioningly. The nurse got down on her knees and asked, "Mark, did your mother to this to you?" That's when I really lost control of myself and cried harder. She held me in her arms for a long time, she and the principal crying with me. I didn't want to tell anyone because I thought the "State" would put me in a foster home.

Dad was away a lot moving families across the United States and Canada. He would be away for months except in the Fall and Winter (November - March). Then he'd be closer to home, but still not home. I know that I was beaten a lot because Dad was away. My grades in school were poor. I didn't keep the apartment clean enough for Mom's "White Glove Inspection." I had to take care of my younger brother, help him to do his homework, do house work, play outside in the front with him, get dinner started or have it ready when Mom got home. I had to make sure that my homework was done and done right. Mom says she helped me many times with homework, but it was by yelling and putting me down.

There were times when I was tired and took a nap after school. I'd oversleep and Mom would pull me off the bed by the collar, wrist or leg and start punching me. Long before the age of 16, I asked Jesus why didn't He take my life when I was in the Sunshine Cottage.

When I graduated from high school in 1968, I got a job at a moving company. I packed, unpacked, loaded and unloaded furniture. My local driving was in a 60-150 mile radius of the office. These were hard hours, but happy ones. I talked to drivers and their families. The families we were moving read all kind of road maps and dreamed of going to all these states, and I dreamed of having my own trucking company. I paid my Mom's room and board until I went to college in 1970.

My relationship is distant with my own two boys. I had to draw from my friend's fathers, uncles, grandfathers to learn how to be a man and a father. Dad wasn't a good role model. He said he loved us, but when he was home he was drunk, slept a lot, and beat Mom. I am 49, married for 19 years, have two children, and am void of real love from my own parents. It's very sad. My children don't want anything to do with me since my wife left me in 1998.

How am I celebrating? I am not in that mess with my mother and I didn't create one in my marriage or on the job or in the church. I am living one of my dreams. I have my own trucking business and I do travel. Another goal that I have is to talk to people on a large or small scale about hope and help. To heal and deal with life's hurt is a must. There is help and hope for you and your loved ones. When you can see the signs, don't turn a deaf ear. Do something positive before they break down your mental health or cause loss of life. Remember that Christ is your healer and your hope.

To Bobby, From Helen

Dear Bobby,

It's so empty here without you. Our daughter is depressed. I am sure wondering where you are. This Sunday was beautiful, but I couldn't seem to get outside. I look out the windows and see the beauty and the birds outside, and yet feel so alone without you.

Nights are the worst, getting in bed, wrapped in my cocoon covers. There's just an aching I feel in my heart, and it's so difficult to sleep without you near me. I don't know how you feel, but I can guess that you share the loneliness. They say I'm experiencing the "grieving process," that change in the relationship happens like a rebirth, and when that happens part of the relationship dies too. But there are moments of hope too, looking forward to a beginning. I am afraid of the pain in change. God willing, these "labor pains" will signify the birth of a renewed love and commitment.

I know what you're thinking I've said my 2500 words. I want to tell you how much I miss you, and hurt for you. There is a soft caring woman behind that iron called strong willed, one who loves you and wants more than ever to be part of your life if you want that too. There's just a wee small voice inside that tells me no matter what happens, positive things are in store for us. They may not be what we expect. For instance–if you choose to go, to leave what we have together, I must find the love to let you go and respect your wishes. That would be very difficult for me–but I sense that in the aftermath of this hurricane, we will find a new way to relate and possess the possibility of finding and sharing love. Risking loss for gain…

The sand hill cranes are calling and singing a lot tonight. I love their song and it seems they are singing just for me – perhaps for us. They must know what we are going through.

The easy path is rarely the one that leads to fulfillment. It is healing we both need now and perhaps taking the time to search within, listening to the still small voice…only then can we sing in harmony.

Your wife,

Helen

KEEPING MY HEAD

Elizabeth's Story

I was born on the tiny island of Barbados. Being the first of four children, I grew up in a fairly 'normal' family setting. Both parents worked very hard to provide the necessities of life and to ensure a sound education for all of us. My mother always felt it was important that her children receive the education that was not afforded herself and my dad. They were not illiterate, though not privileged to attend high school.

Growing up, I was always a very contented kid. Some have said I was a little spoiled, being the first child and first grandchild for about three years. I attended the Barbados Seventh-day Adventist Secondary School where I received my formal education. After graduation, I enrolled in nursing school, a career choice that I thought would stay with me all my life. Although I was accepted, I was too young and had to wait for a later class. While I waited for my age to catch up with my brain I taught at the neighborhood elementary school. I did not know that I had such a love for small children. Somehow though I never felt inclined to enroll in teacher college because I was waiting to go to nursing school. After waiting for six months, I completed only half of a three-year program because my aunt sponsored me to Canada with the hopes that I would study nursing in this country. She believed that the prospects would be much better there. I arrived in Canada in February, 1975 and was very intrigued by a new place (I still wonder every winter why I am here).

I immediately started working on my enrollment to college for nurses training but was unsuccessful, the prerequisites dictated that I upgrade my science subjects. Meanwhile, I worked at a nursing home at night as I attended day school. While at college I met a young man who is now my husband. After the marriage my dream of becoming a nurse died. He insisted that we relocate to the suburbs because work was better there for him. Shortly after he opened his own business and I became the secretary a job that I had absolutely no training for, but I picked it up very quickly.

At the age of twenty-two my first son was born and I became a "stay-at-home" mum and secretary–nothing really wrong with that–except that this sweet, loving man became very abusive. About two years into the marriage he was diagnosed as Paranoid Schizophrenic after I had to be admitted to a psychiatric hospital near the point of a nervous breakdown. Coping with this information and his behavior was not easy. However, I determined in my heart that I would try everything in my power to get the physical abuse to stop. This was accomplished through the courts in1981. I then determined in my heart that the truth never changes so I would not let him break my spirit with his accusations. I started back to church after a five year absence. There I met new friends and formed new relationships. It was there that I had a life outside my home, that I could have an active part in an organization. I took on the responsibility of Children's Ministries Coordinator. On Sabbath mornings, three of the children were my own. I was in the nursery anyway, so why not? This job brought me a great sense of belonging. Planning programs and delegating responsibility brought out a side of me that I did not even know existed. As programs became successful I gained more confidence in myself. Many other people gained confidence in me and I tried to live up to that expectation. For ten years I held that position and was recognized last year by the church body with a engraved plaque for dedicated service.

I found this book, "Verbal Abuse Survivors Speak Out" to be very informative and very easy to read. It was one of the books in my "self help" recovery program because I was a victim of spousal abuse. In the late seventies and early eighties no one talked about their bedroom business like they do today, so I suffered a great deal in silence with small children. I thought about leaving many times, but where would I go? How would I support myself? What hurt even deeper was when people would say to me "Oh you are so lucky, you don't have to work." Little did they know I worked harder than any of them without a dime or thank you. Many times I wished that the behavior I saw exhibited in my spouse to family and friends would be mine for one hour, at least.

This made it very difficult to talk about, even if I could talk to any one. If they knew us they would never believe me and I could not risk that, so I said nothing. Obvious trauma to the body has a name, we call it battering or physical abuse. It is highly visible, pictures can be taken for a later use, and even then there is denial that it ever happened. The wounds heal without a scar sometimes, but the wounded "inner child" most times cannot be comforted.

Many times as I read the book I found myself checking the names of the survivors who wrote to the author to be sure that in the midst of my confusion I did not write the letter. Word for word I could identify with them: the belittling comments like "You can never do anything right," "you're so sensitive," "what would you do without me," "you'll never be anything without me," and the list goes on and on. However, I look on the bright side because I have been validated for the good and capable person that I am.

I knew that I was not crazy, so I concentrated on the healing and recovery sections of the book. I found "The Sixty Minute Me and Self-Esteem" in this book particularly helpful. This chapter deals with building self-esteem, restoring confidence in yourself by using affirmations each day like, "I know I have the power to succeed" which are all listed in the chapter "Affirmations."

I was still determined that I would be educated no matter what. So I took a number of correspondence courses: high school diploma, accounting, bookkeeping and computer programming, especially after home computers became a mass market product. I read many books on various subjects, concentrating mainly on those that dealt with spousal relationships. I learned many valuable lessons. I learned that I was not the only one with this problem. I also learned that I could not change anyone who was in denial. This gave me tremendous courage as I set out to rebuild my confidence and self-esteem. My motto came from a poem I learned when I was a little girl. I cannot remember the title, the author nor any more of it but it went like this, "If you can keep your head when all around is losing theirs and blaming it on you...then you will be a man, my son."* I still cope by keeping my head. Twenty years and five children later I am still chasing my dream of obtaining a degree. It is not easy for me, but I am enjoying it. My children and their friends have become my fan club. I am devoted to teaching my children and other young people at the same church that abuse of any kind is wrong. I have adopted the philosophy that I should not criticize anything that I cannot fix. I cannot fix the past generations of abusers. However, I will do whatever I can to teach my children (the future spouses) what is acceptable and appropriate behavior. I strongly believe that if they are encouraged to respect themselves and others, and to be considerate and compassionate, especially with their siblings, it should be easier for them to carry this behavior into adulthood. I urge them always to stay in school and try to excel academically, not only for financial independence but as a means of self fulfillment.

Presently I am seeing a psychiatrist once a month, not because I am ill but because I have come to the awareness that I need a professional in the mix of all the people who help me "keep my head' in this world. I am hoping when I graduate from the university I will be able to teach or counsel the youth as I have grown so fond of them over the years.

By staying in touch with my true feelings and being my own good parent to my inner child, taking care of my own needs first or buying myself things for no reason, I am coping much better without leaving the relationship. Someday I hope my spouse will come to the awareness of his illness and seek the necessary treatment, but until then I have to be me–a free spirit.

**From the poem, "If for Boys" by Rudyard Kipling.*

THE TRUTH ABOUT YOUR THOUGHTS AND FEELINGS

When you think of the wisdom and scope of God's plan, fall down on your knees and pray that out of His glorious, unlimited resources He will give you the Mighty inner strengthening of His Holy Spirit.

Pray that Christ will be more and more at home in your heart, living within you as you trust in Him.

May your roots go down deep into the soil of His marvelous love; and may you be able to understand, as all His children should, how long, how wide, how deep, and how high His love really is; and experience this love for yourself, though it is so great that you will never see the end of it or fully know or understand it.

And so at last you will be filled up with Him.

Glory be to God, who by His mighty power at work within you, is able to do far more than you would ever dare to ask or even dream of–infinitely beyond your highest prayer, desire, thought, or hope" Ephesians 3:14-20.

MY THOUGHTS AND FEELINGS

Sometimes I am so broken, I don't feel pain,
My life is messed up, I want to start it all over again.

Sometimes I get angry with Your apparent lack of care
It seems that You abandon me. Are You really here?
Sometimes when people reject me I wish I was never born.
I get hurt by their ridicule, contempt and scorn.

Sometimes when I am lonely I want to see Your face,
I want to know You smile at me. I want to feel Your embrace.

Sometimes I get so very weak, I am ready to give up
Because I don't feel that You support me just enough.

Sometimes I wonder why I keep trying to live by Your rules
When it's so much easier to use the devil's tools.

Sometimes I wonder why I keep helping, sharing, and giving to others
Yet when I need a helping hand, no one ever bothers.

Sometimes I get overwhelmed with depression, pain and sorrow,
I don't want to even think about a tomorrow.

Why don't You reward me for serving You?
Why don't You comfort me when I am sad?
Why don't You answer when I call?
Why don't You fix me when I'm bad?

-Mable Dunbar

His Thoughts & Feelings

Just now He speaks to me:
I am, therefore you are
I understand
I hear you
I see you
I want you
I love you
I died for you
I am with you
I will help you
I will save you
I think of you
I feel for you
Always.
And if you don't have the strength to seek me.
I will seek you
Always!"

-Mable Dunbar

CHAPTER FOUR

Our Right to Do

"Being confident of this very thing, that He which hath begun a good work in you will perform it until the day of Jesus Christ" Philipians 1:6.

"I can do all things through Christ who strengthens me" Philipians 4:8.

My greatest accomplishment in life has been to recognize that God loves me, and that I am in His plans. It does not matter how I was born, or what people think of me. I am special to Him. I pray fervently and purposefully each day to keep my connection with my Creator and Designer. I explore and experiment with my abilities. I surround myself with people who give me positive and constructive messages. I give myself positive messages. I deserve to be here. I deserve to be happy. I deserve to shine. I deserve to be alive. I deserve to succeed.

HOW WE LIMIT OUR DOING

We perform in ways that are not consistent with our gifts, skills, and talents.

Sometimes we are afraid to let others know that we are gifted because we feel they will reject us. We do not let them see our abilities in certain areas because they might get jealous of us, they might exploit us, they might ridicule us, or they might see us as not needing them to do anything for us.

We may get involved in too much to escape success, responsibility, accountability, or criticism.

Whenever we reach a point in our lives where we can be successful we perform in ways that will prevent us from achieving that success because we are afraid that we will be noticed. We sabotage our success. We are afraid that if we don't remain successful, people will laugh at us, criticize us or not support us. We tell ourselves that we can't; therefore, we don't try.

We may do nothing to avoid failure.

We rationalize that it is better to be inactive rather than fail. If we do nothing we will not be seen. However, our inactivity leads to stagnation, and we begin to feel as if we are of no value because we are not making a contribution to our family or to society. We feel guilty and ashamed of our lack of initiative, but our fear of failure outweighs our desire to do.

We act dependent, needy,and passive instead of exploring or creating.

We feel inadequate. Rather than search out new ways to develop and expand our talents we do nothing. Rather than try new methods to accomplish our goals we do nothing. Rather than set goals, we continue doing the same thing over and over again in the same way with worse results. We get stuck in the same routine becoming powerless to make changes.

We base our actions on what others expect of us, instead of what God expects of us, or of what we expect of ourselves.

Our activities are based on what other people want us to do. These activities might be painful for us. They might be contrary to our personal and religious values. But we are desperate for attention from someone, anyone. So we continue these behaviors, even if they are destructive to us and those in our care.

We act timid or unapproachable to avoid commitment.

There are people in our lives who really like us, and want to get to know us better. But because we feel that we are not good enough, we put up barriers to drive them away. We sabotage healthy relationships. We act shy, aggressive or self-sufficient to prevent them from getting too close. We are afraid to make any commitment to them because we don't feel that we can live up to their expectations or keep them interested in us.

AFFIRMATION OF OUR DOING

Fact:

I have the right to maintain supportive/productive relationships.

Message:

I am a special human being, created in the image of God. I will allow myself to be open to those relationships that support and motivate me to excel mentally, physically, spiritually, and socially.

Affirmation:

Two people are always better off than one because they can work together and enjoy each other's company. If one of them falls, the other can help him up. But I pity the man who walks alone, because when he falls, he has not one to help him...Two can resist an attack better than one trying to do it alone. A rope made from three strands is much stronger than a rope made from one" Ecclesiastes 4:9,10, 12. "Those who love You and keep Your commandments are my closest friends" Psalm 119:64.

Fact:

I have the right to terminate unsupportive/unproductive relationships.

Message:

If I have relationships that are not supportive or productive, I will leave them. I do not have to feel guilty because I will be taking care of myself.

Affirmation:

"Happy is the man (woman) who doesn't take advice from the ungodly, who doesn't participate in the ways of wicked men (women) and who doesn't criticize them" Psalm 1:1.

"Don't go into partnership with those who believe differently from you. It won't work. How can right have fellowship with wrong? What does light have in common with darkness?" 2 Corinthians 6:14. "Even though my father and mother might abandon me, the Lord will love and care for me" Psalm 28:10.

Fact:
I have the right to find new footing and become grounded.

Message:
If I find myself in relationships, places or situations that make me feel unstable or unsafe I can explore new options.

Affirmation:
"If anyone accepts Christ into his life He's remade from within. Old values pass away and new values take over. He's a new creation, a new and different person!" 2 Corinthians 5:17.

Fact:
I have the right to be active and mobile.

Message:
Sometimes I have the instinct to do certain things or go certain places. But my fear of the unknown keeps me from acting on my urges. As I develop my relationship with God, He will direct my instincts. I will not be afraid to get involved with activities that help me to grow, help others, and glorify Him.

Affirmation:
"Whatever you do, give it everything you've got and enjoy it. Once you die, there's no activity, thought, knowledge, or wisdom in the grave where you'll eventually go" Ecclesiastes 9:10.

"After all is said and done, there is only one thing that really matters: Respect your heavenly Father and do what He says. That is all that matters. God knows what is best for you. His will is written out in the Ten Commandments. He will eventually judge everything we have done in this life, including every secret thing, whether it was good or bad" Ecclesiastes 12:13, 14.

Fact:

I have the right to set limits and boundaries.

Message:

I can decide just how far I will let someone enter my personal space. I won't let anyone treat me with disrespect. I will not allow anyone to talk to me in a way that is demeaning or embarrassing. I will let them know that there is a line that I will not allow them to cross when it comes to my well-being. If they cross that line, I will remove myself from their presence.

Affirmation:

"In You, Lord, do I put my trust; don't let me down. Deliver me for your righteousness' sake. Please listen to me and save me. Continue to be my Rock, my refuge where I can always go. Command Your angels to rescue me. You alone are my Rock and my Fortress. Deliver me, O my God, from the hand of the wicked, from those evil and cruel men. You have always been my hope, O Lord. I have trusted You since my youth. You've protected me since the day I was born and were with me even when I came out of my mother's womb. Thank you for all You have done for me; I will praise You forever" Psalm 71:1-6.

Fact:

I have the right to make decisions.

Message:

I will seek to understand myself. I will explore what it is I want to do with my life. I will make sure to rely on competent and qualified people to give me advice. I will ask many questions and continue to do so until I find the answers. I will make the best decisions that are right for me.

Affirmation:

"Lord, You have given us Your laws and told us to keep them. How I wish that my nature were inclined to do what You ask me to do. Then I wouldn't feel ashamed of myself when I consider Your commandments. But I will praise You with my whole heart as I learn more about the rightness of Your law. I will keep Your statues; only stay close to me and help me" Psalm 119:5-8.

Fact:

I have the right to make and honor my own priorities

Message:

When it comes to my priorities, I can honor them and not feel guilty. I am just as important as anyone else: my children, my husband, my significant other, my parents, my siblings, my friends, etc. So I can do things for myself that will help me feel good about myself.

Affirmation:

"Each one of you is a manager of some of God's gifts, so use those gifts to help others like good stewards, administering God's grace in its various forms. For instance, whoever preaches should preach the word of God with conviction. Whoever serves should do it with the strength that God has given him, so that God will be praised through Jesus Christ. All glory and power and dominion belong to God both now and forever" 1 Peter 4:10, 11.

Fact:

I have the right to be quiet, relaxed and playful.

Message:

I need to remind myself every day that it is okay to do some fun things. I can relax and take out time to enjoy the beauty of nature, a good book, some friends, a bubble bath, a manicure, a new hairdo, etc. Sometimes I might want to be quiet, and just listen to my inner being and nurture myself. I can laugh and play. I can take out time to enjoy being alive in God.

Affirmation:

"A (woman) should be happy and enjoy(her) family, (her) friends, and (her) food. These things will cheer (her) on (her) way through all the days God has given (her)" Ecclesiastes 8: 15.

Fact:

I have the right to forgive myself and trust God for healing.

Message:

Because He has promised that He is "faithful and just to forgive me of my sins, and to cleanse me from all unrighteousness"(1 John 1:9), I will forgive myself for all the wrong that I have done to myself and others, and what I have allowed others to do to me. I will stop rehearsing all of my faults and concentrate on the good person that I am and the good things I have done. As I continue my journey I will trust God to heal me.

Affirmation:

"He has forgiven your sins and healed your diseases" Psalm 103:2. "Lord, heal me, and I will be healed. Save me, and I will be saved. You are my hope, the One I will praise" Jeremiah 17:4.

"I will heal your wounds and restore your health" Jeremiah 30:17. "Prayer is the answer to every problem in life. It puts us in tune with divine wisdom which know not to adjust everything perfectly. So often we do not pray in certain situations, because from our standpoint the outlook is hopeless. But nothing is impossible with God. No human relation is too strained for God to bring about reconciliation and understanding. No habit is so deep rooted that it cannot be overcome. No one is so weak that he cannot be strong. No one is so ill that he cannot be healed. No mind is so dull that it cannot be made brilliant. Whatever we need or desire, if we trust God He will supply it. If anything is causing worry and anxiety, let's stop rehearing the difficulty and trust God for healing, love and power" *Review & Herald*, October 7, 1865.

Fact:

I have the right to do things as many times as I need to.

Message:

Even if I fail in certain areas, I can try over and over again until I succeed. If I don't succeed, it's still okay. I will try something else. I will not waste time trying to do what I don't have the gifts, talents or interests to do. I have a creative side that has limitless potential. I will explore it.

Affirmation:

"I know that You will help me because I try to do what is right. Please keep me close to You forever" Psalm 41:12.

"If those who depend on Him do stumble, they won't stay down, because the Lord will help them up" Psalm 37:24.

Fact:

I have the right to know God for myself and develop my own personal relationship with Him in my own time, and in my own way.

Message:

I will not allow anyone to force me to see God through their eyes. As I develop my relationship with Him I will depend on Him to guide me as I deepen my commitment to Him. I will refrain from letting others dictate how many times I should pray, what I should study, and how I should worship Him. I will not allow anyone to force me into a mold that will prevent me from experiencing the spontaneous joy of being totally surrendered to Him. I will ask Him daily to direct my plans so that He will be reflected in my being, thinking, feeling, and doing.

Affirmation:

"Then the Lord said to me, 'Don't let the wise man glory in his wisdom nor the strong man in his strength nor the rich man in his riches, but let those who glory, glory in this, that they know me and understand that I am the Lord, the One who is steadfast in love. I delight in being kind, righteous and just toward all" Jeremiah 9:24-25.

"I am the Lord your God, the One who teaches you what is right, who directs you in the way you should go" Isaiah 48:17.

Exercise #1- Exploring My Actions

DIRECTIONS: Consider all that you have been told to do and what you are expected to do. Take a few minutes and answer the following questions.

What does God want me to do?

What does my family want me to do?

What do I want to do?

What is best for me to do?

How can I do it?

Exercise #2 - Hypothetically Speaking

Here is something you might want to do with a trusted friend.

You are a gifted and talented person who has much to offer to the world. You just invented a new and efficient way to let everyone know that you have discovered the cure for sorrow, pain, and all forms of suffering. But people are very busy and don't have time to listen to what you have to say. What will you do to get their attention?

I will ______________________________

The cure for the ills of the world is JESUS. Share Him with someone today.

EMPTIED OF GARBAGE...FILLED WITH HIS LIMITLESS LOVE

Cynthia's Story

My mother was a Newfoundlander and my father was French/Italian who was orphaned and abandoned at age three. Both my parents had difficult backgrounds and carried that baggage into their marriage. My mother became pregnant in their first year of marriage. My father, who was emotionally starved and needed a "mother type," became very jealous of the four children that came within seven years. As a result, my mother would not show us any affection and neglected us emotionally. She withdrew from my father and thought sex was disgusting. Their war zone became the marital bed.

My father verbally abused her after we kids were in bed. Very rarely did we see him abuse her physically until we reached our teens. We'd lay in bed at nights and hear the most degrading, disgusting, vile words hurled at our mother, words designed to shred her self-esteem and her heart into pieces.

But this was not enough of an outlet for his anger and frustration. Parental "discipline" became his other outlet for venting. When did the abuse start? My earliest memories start around age five. For our childhood misdemeanors, my older sister and I would be stripped naked from the waist down, laid over the back of an armchair and whipped with a thick leather belt. My father was forever punching me in the face and I can remember frequent bloody noses or his long finger nails raking up the back of my neck to grasp the nape hair and then walking me around the house on my tiptoes pleading for mercy.

Mealtimes were the most miserable time of day. Someone always "got it," one of Dad's famous back handers or "love pats" as he called them. One of us would get smashed across the face and sent flying backwards off the chair. If we didn't want to eat all our dinner, we had his long nails pinch into our cheeks to pry our mouths open into which he would then stuff us so full of food we thought we would suffocate.

My worst memory is from a mealtime, when I was about nine. We had been playing outside energetically and were called in for dinner. I was last to come and headed for the kitchen sink for water as I was so thirsty. Dad told me to sit. I said I needed a drink and kept heading for the sink. Wrong move. He flew off his chair in a rage and ran to me, slammed me across the face with his fist. I literally saw stars, blacked out for a moment and fell on to the stove. The blood was gushing all over my shirt and when my head hit the stove, I fell to the floor.

My mother never usually intervened, but this time she must have been afraid for me because she leaped off her chair to stop Dad. This enraged him, that she should dare to interfere. He grabbed a handful of my hair and picked me up off the floor like a rag doll. He shook me in mid-air with the blood spattering everywhere in front of my mother, taunting her. She started to pound his back with her fists to make him let me go. He dropped me to the floor, but didn't release my hair. I was dragged around the house, bouncing off door frames and furniture...mother was ripping his shirt off his back, pounding on him and screaming. Finally I was thrown up against the wall under the bathroom sink and left to sob.

My mother came back with my pajamas to clean me up. She washed up the blood, brushed my hair (which came out in clumps), and changed me into my pajamas. There were no comforting hugs, no kisses, and no dinner. I was beaten and sent to bed with no dinner–all because I wanted a drink of water.

These kinds of scenes got worse as we got older. My older sister and brother would fight back eventually...overturning furniture, breaking things and smashing each other. All of us turned to drinking and drugs at very early ages to feel something other than the pain: my sisters and I each at 14, my brother at 12.

When I couldn't be high, I lost myself in my studies...anything to keep my mind pre-occupied and busy. I maintained honor grades all through school. I was determined that I would escape from home early. I did five years of high school in four and got accepted into the university by age 17. I left home a month after I turned 18 to start at the university. In retrospect, I was emotionally unequipped to be on my own that early. I looked for love in all the wrong places.

By the end of my first year at the university I found myself without direction, involved with a man equally without direction, and unfortunately, pregnant. I don't know what attracted me to him. Maybe it was his lost little puppy look, thinking he was someone I could help and take care of, but underneath the surface, he was entirely different.

I married a man much like my father, angry and violent. He was unfaithful during my pregnancy and was verbally abusive. I heard things spoken to me that were much the same in tone and vileness as those I heard spoken to my mother....things that stole whatever sense of self-esteem and womanhood I had.

His physical abuse started when our son was about six months old, at which time I had started a job as a teller in a bank. I had also resumed university studies by correspondence. He resented any attempts of mine to improve, to be independent, to use my mind. He would first accuse me of unfaithfulness with the bank manager or with the professors, none of which were true. When I would deny those things, he would get angrier until he would lose control.

I tried many times to escape the relationship because of some innate God-given belief that I could find happiness. I also had such a deep awakening about what love felt like when I had my children...at last I could love and be loved unconditionally.

At times, I had help from co-workers and friends, social workers and a woman's shelter. I would move to other cities and he would follow me. I wound up pregnant a second time during a brief reconciliation and he informed me afterwards that he had sabotaged the birth control.

He left me for another woman when I was about four months pregnant with our daughter. She was my friend's roommate. My friend called me up to say he had been with this woman, so when he showed up at my door, I had his things waiting on the doorstep.

He came back when I was seven months pregnant, determined to make me pay for kicking him out. He lured me into the basement on the pretense of me helping him find some things that he had left there in boxes. When I went downstairs, I knew I was in dire trouble when I saw his blanched face and the darkness in his eyes. He pulled out handcuffs and cuffed my hands behind my back. I couldn't struggle too well in my condition. He stuffed my mouth with a sock so that I couldn't cry out during the sexual assault and awaken our son. When he ungagged me, I said that if I lost the baby I would charge him with murder. He fled. And so began what I call my "lost years."

He stalked and terrorized me for years after that. The justice system can never protect a woman from a man like that. He spied on me and tried to break into my apartment. One time he kidnapped me off the street as I walked to work. He threatened to murder me. He'd rape me. He'd beat on me. The court ordered me to give my children to him every other weekend and that terrified me. One weekend he grabbed me as I dropped the kids off at his apartment and dragged me to his bedroom and began to try to rape me. My five-year-old son saw what was happening and went to the kitchen, got a knife, came to the end of the bed with the knife poised to plunge into the waterbed until his daddy let his mommy go. My child saved me and I agonized over having to leave them there with that man. There was nothing I could do but escape and cry in agony all weekend. It wasn't until he found another woman years later that he left me alone.

There were a few times in my life that I prayed to God. My mother had made my older sister and I go to Sunday school for a few years and I knew about God and Jesus. I went to a Pentecostal Pathfinders group when I was eight or nine, and they talked about Jesus' love a lot. How I wanted to be loved! One night they had an altar call for us children...anyone who wanted to give their heart to Jesus. How I wanted Jesus to love me, and if that meant I had to give my heart first, then I would. So I obeyed the alter call.

I remember that we were given the opportunity afterwards to select a gift to commemorate that moment. I walked the length of the table and tried to select my gift. I then saw a small plaster plaque of Jesus picking up the lost little lamb. That was me and Jesus. The next week, I had hands laid on me again just to make absolutely sure that I had given my heart to Jesus and that I was His.

I prayed during my teen years for God to prevent me from running away from home. I just wanted to stay long enough to finish school. With His strength I did. I prayed during both pregnancies, arms wrapped around my belly praying for my unborn children to be strong and healthy, for me to hold on and be a good mother. God took care of my babies. Amongst the alcohol and drugs, He still cared for me. Despite the sexual promiscuity, He still cared for me. He stayed by my side through 14 years of raising my babies as a single parent, going to night school and working during the day.

I didn't really understand what a personal relationship with Jesus meant until I became an Adventist. I was baptized in 1987 with both my children in the baptistry with me. We found God as a family.

At times through the years, we would have to head into counseling as a family or just for me or one of the children. We all suffered great emotional pain, deep resentment and anger. My daughter was so shy. By age five she was so introverted she began regressing into bed-wetting/daywetting and not talking to anyone except through me. The doctor thought she was displaying symptoms of sexual abuse, but we could never prove it was her father. I believe that the ongoing fear and terror we lived through for those early years took a toll on her. She would freak out when any man went near her.

My son became angry and aggressive. Although the teachers never caught him, they would always say that there were constant complaints about him pinching, kicking or hitting from the other children. He went into play therapy. He saw his father beating me from the time he was in diapers, though he says he doesn't remember even the incident with the knife and the waterbed.

Nothing seemed to help him. Of course, it never helped that his father constantly put me down in front of him, called me crazy, and always tried to get him to go live with him. By the time my son hit adolescence and the turbulent hormones, the stress of years of single parenthood had robbed me of any capacity to deal with him.

Our relationship deteriorated into yelling and arguing, ending up with him saying how much he hated me and wanted to live with his dad. I tried more counseling, but by the time he was 16 he hated me so much that he wouldn't listen to reason. He went to live with his dad. I was devastated and cried for months. He is there to this day, and I pray for him always.

For me...well drugs, alcohol and men were always a way of escape from thinking about the pain and my life. When I wasn't working or with the children, then I had to be high....especially on those weekends when the kids were with their dad. It was the only way I could handle it, handle talking to him. Then when I gave my heart to Jesus again as an adult, and gave up those behaviors, others set in.

I developed an eating disorder, bulimia. I got back into counseling again. The church had a good health message and I had to get myself healthy inside and out...not just physically and spiritually, but emotionally too. Once over that, I ended up in counseling again during the rough years with my son. I had to learn to let go of the bitterness and anger.

Unfortunately, I wasn't emotionally healed and desperate for some earthly love and I became involved/got married to a man who again I thought I could take care of. My unhealthy perspective about relationships, and bad role models led me down the wrong path. I heard the warning signals from God, but I ignored them and got married after a six month courtship. Six weeks after marriage, he was sleeping on the couch. He was an angry man and would pick fights over anything and storm out on the couch. When charges from a pornography shop appeared on my credit card statement and I confronted him with them, he lied and said they were nothing. His addiction to pornography made him guilty, and his guilt made his anger escalate. He took this anger out on me. I kept warning him that he was pushing all the wrong triggers and one day the love would just die within me.

I got an offer to transfer to another city, and he encouraged me to take the job. I moved and he showed up to help me settle in the rented house. He got angrier and angrier about every little thing, cursing and swearing, until he threw a step ladder at me across the kitchen in front of my daughter. He then stormed out saying he would never live with me there and left to go back to the other city. At that moment the love died and I knew we would never get back together.

I spent a few more years healing and being loved by my Lord, church family and friends. I concentrated on my career and it took off. I have also continued my schooling and any effort at self-improvement to this day. I am presently a banker in Canada and have a business degree from a university.

Three years ago I met a gentle, loving man at church. We got married. We are approaching our second anniversary. What a difference love can make in a relationship. What a difference the Lord can make. I envisioned the perfect relationship from all the things that the Bible had to say, and it's almost perfect. That's not to say that we both don't have baggage we're still trying to leave at the foot of the cross...it can be a struggle sometimes to leave it there and not bring it between us. But with the strength of the Lord it can be done. With the help of a pastor, friends and family, it can be done. With counseling it can be done. I believe that "I can do all things through Christ."

What really keeps me going is being able to help others. I started a support group in our church for single parent families. Most of these women or their children have been abused in some way. The Lord has shown me that we must care and love one another, especially when our sisters or brothers are hurting...and especially when children are involved. That's when they need us most, whether they are Christians or not. It's amazing...I looked for love all my life, just for me. It's hard to believe that the Lord has fulfilled my life and given me so much love, that I now have a love cup that's overflowing to others. This hardly seems possible.

I want everyone to know that God and Jesus do not want anyone to remain in an abusive relationship. Yes, God hates divorce, but he had to provide the means for escape in this sick, sinful world from a sick, abusive relationship. God wants the best and the ideal for us, but when Satan has taken control of abusive individuals who are in our lives, we must escape. We are told to flee from Satan.

And flee you must, for your sake and the sake of your children. It will take you years to heal and learn to trust again. It will take a long time for your children to heal. It may not come until they are adults themselves. If your husband seeks help and heals, then thank God for this miracle. Be advised that his healing will take years too....don't be too quick to reconcile.

God wants a man to love his wife the way Jesus loves the church...so much so that he would die for his wife rather than let any harm come to her or harm her himself. When in an abusive relationship, ask yourself, "What would Jesus do?" If our gracious Savior prevented the stoning of the prostitute, He wants to prevent your abuse too. He will provide a way of escape. When He provides it, you need to take it.

Talk to people. It will be hard, but talk. Contact a woman's shelter and speak to professional counselors. Speak to women who have gone through and come out on the other side. Reach out.

Set goals, educate yourself or get a job. Concentrate on the you of the future. Don't get stuck in the past. Don't get stuck in the victim mentality. Move on and let the nightmares gradually dissipate. Believe me, they will.

Love your children. They have seen and heard enough. Don't yell at them. Don't hit them. Don't give them reason to fear you. When you find yourself losing control in times of stress, set up a support system to either call someone or go somewhere. Don't take it out on the children.

Trust in God and love Him with all your heart, with all your mind, with your body, with all your soul. Pour out your agonies of spirit and mind to Him. My favorite verse is Psalm 18:6. "In my distress I called upon the Lord, and cried unto my God: He heard my voice out of his temple, and my cry came before Him, even into His ears." He wants us to cry all the pain, the anger, the bitterness, the hate out to Him. I have walked through forests screaming my pain out to Him...in my distress, I cried out unto the Lord and He heard me. I emptied all the garbage from my heart. Once my heart was emptied of all the pain, He poured His limitless love into it and made me whole.

King David knew how to cry unto the Lord. So many psalms start in agony of spirit and end praising the goodness of the Lord. That is God's gift to you when you come through the other side...limitless love and an abundant life.

THE TRUTH ABOUT YOUR DOING

"Just as you've always obeyed God, not only when I was with you, but even more when I was away, continue doing so.

Put the salvation you received from Christ to work in your daily life, with humility of mind, all the time recognizing that it is God who is at work in you.

He is the One who energizes your will and enables you to obey Him. So be grateful for what He is doing for you and whatever you do for Him, do it without arguing and complaining. Everything you do should be blameless, innocent and above reproach. You are God's children living in a corrupt world. You are lights in the darkness, like **stars lighting up the night sky**" Philippians 2:12-15.

Lord,

Grant me the serenity

To accept the things I cannot change,

The courage to change the things I can

And the wisdom to know the difference.

-St. Francis of Assisi

C H A P T E R   F I V E

Truth Triumphant

Every human being created in the image of God is endowed with a power akin to that of the Creator:Individuality, Power to Think and to Do
Ellen G. White, Education, *p. 17.*

You are special to the Lord (Zechariah 2:8). He gives you power as you journey through recovery, renewal and healing (Malachi 4:2). He reminds you that He is your Counselor (Isaiah 9:6), Friend (Luke 7:34), Brother, Sister, Mother (Matthew 12:50), Husband (Isaiah 54:5), and sends you His Comforter (John 16:7). He is your Guide (Isaiah 58:11), Shield (Psalm 28:7), Defender (Psalm 20:1), and Deliverer (Psalm 144:2). He cares for you and seeks to draw nearer and dearer to you. Your value lies not in where you came from, your family of origin, your educational background, race, culture, religious persuasion or socio-economic status, but in your connection with Him.

> *"On the way to the Garden of Gethsemane Jesus saw in the moonlight a vine with a dead branch. He pointed to it and said,'I'm like a grapevine planted in my Father's vineyard, and He's the gardener. You are the branches. If there is a branch on the vine that does not bear fruit, He will cut it off; those branches do not bear fruit He will keep on trimming so they can bear more fruit.*
>
> *Your characters have been shaped already because I shared the word of God with you and you accepted it as such. Stay with me and I'll stay with you. Just like branches can't bear fruit on their own unless they're attached to the vine, neither can you bear heavenly fruit unless you're attached to Me.*
>
> *I am the true vine and you are my branches. If you remain in Me and I remain in you, you will bear much fruit. Without Me, you can't do a thing. If you detach yourself from Me, your spirituality will shrivel up and die, just as a branch will shrivel up when it's cut off from the vine. Together with the other dead branches, it will be put on the brush pile and burned.*
>
> *If you remain committed to Me and my words become a part of you, then you can ask the Father to give you what you need to produce fruit and He'll give it to you'" John 15:1-7.*

Without Him, you are nothing. But with Him you are everything and can do anything!

Conclusion

Maybe your family of origin, friends, and circumstances caused you to limit yourself. The reality is God has made and ordained you to be an empowered, dynamic, and fulfilled person in Him. So you never need to feel abandoned, rejected, inadequate or alone. You belong to the family of God and His family:

> "The Lord says, "Listen to me....You are my people. I have chosen you to be mine. I am the Lord who created you, who formed you in the womb. I will help you. Don't be afraid. You are my servant, my chosen people whom I love. I will give water to the thirsty land and make streams flow on the dry ground. I will pour out my Spirit on your children and my blessings on your offspring. They will spring up and grow like well-watered grass in a meadow, like willows next to flowing streams. One by one my people will say, 'I belong to the Lord.' One by one others will come and say, 'I am joining the Lord's people....' Each one will write the sign of the Lord on his hand and will become part of the family of God" Isaiah 44:1-5.

> "You are my people. I created you. I called you out for my glory" Isaiah 43:7.

Glorify Him in your being, personal power, ability to think and feel, and ability to do. Even though your past might not have been the way you would have liked it to be, your future can be glorious in Him! Blessings and love to you.

Book List

Dan Allender, The Wounded Heart. NavPress: Colorado, 1990.

Neil T. Anderson, The Bondage Breaker: Overcoming Negative Thoughts, Irrational Feelings, Habitual Sins. Harvest House Publishers: Oregon, 1993.

Gilbert V. Boers, Turn Your Hearts Into Healing. Fleming H. Revel: New Jersey, 1991.

Rich Buhler, New Choices New Boundaries: How to Make Decisions That are Emotionally and Spiritually Nourishing for Yourself and Others. Thomas Nelson Publishers: Nashville, 1991.

Rich Buhler, Pain and Pretending: Discovering the Causes of Your Co-Dependency. Thomas Nelson Publishers: Nashville, 1991.

Dr. Henry Cloud, Changes That Heal: How to Understand Your Past to Ensure a Healthier Future. Zondervan Publishing House: Michigan, 1992.

Barbara Couden, Understanding Intimate Violence, Review and Herald: Maryland, 1999.

Dr. Susan Forward, Toxic Parents: Overcoming Their Hurtful Legacy and Reclaiming Your life. Bantam Books: New York, 1989.

Lynn Heitritter & Jeanette Vought, Helping Victums of Sexual Abuse. Bethany House Publishers: Minnesota, 1989.

Catherine Clark Kroeger & James R. Beck, Women, Abuse, and the Bible: How Scripture Can Be Used to Hurt or Heal. Baker Books: Michigan, 1996.

Gregory L, Jantz, Healing the Scars of Emotional Abuse. Fleming H. Revell: Michigan, 1995.

Grace Ketterman, Verbal Abuse: Healing the Hidden Wound. Servant Publications: Michigan, 1992.

Ron Potter-Efron & Pat Potter-Efron, Letting Go of Anger. New Hambingers Publications, Inc.: California, 1995.

Ron and Karen Flowers, Peace and Healing. Making Homes Abuse Free. Advent*Source*: Nebraska, 1996.

Ron and Nancy Rockey, Belonging: Overcoming Rejection and Discovering the Freedom of Acceptance. Pacific Press Publishing Association: Idaho, 1998.

Dr. Gary Rosberg, Choosing To Love Again: Restoring Broken Relationships. Focus on the Family Publishing: Colorado, 1992.

David Seamands, Healing For Damaged Emotions: Recovering From the Memories that Cause Pain. Chariot Victor Publishing: Colorado, 1969.

Dr. Charles L. Whitfield, Healing the Child Within: Discovery and Recovery for Adult Children of Dysfunctional Families. Health Communications, Inc: Florida, 1987.

Organizations

Listing of an organization does not imply any recommendation or warranty, expressed, or implied, of the professional or competence of a listed organization or their staff.

Center for the Prevention of Sexual and Domestic Violence (CPSDV)

Educational resource working specifically with religious communities on issues of sexual abuse and domestic violence.

Contact:
2400 45th Street #10
Seattle, WA 98103
Phone: 206-634-1903
www.cpsdv.org

Life Skills International

Offers a program whose focus is to stop domestic violence by bringing the perpetrator to accountability and provide skills for both the perpetrator and the victim to break the cycle of violence.

Contact:
P.O. Box 31227
Aurora, CO 80041-1227
Phone: 303-340-0598

National Association for Christian Recovery

A coalition of ministries dedicated to helping the Christian community become a safe and helpful place for people recovering from addiction, abuse or trauma.

Contact:
P.O. Box 215
Brea, CA 92822-0215
Phone: 714-529-6227
www.christianrecovery.com

National Coalition Against Domestic Violence (NCADV)

Grassroots nonprofit membership organization working to end violence in the lives of women and children. Provide a national network for state coalitions and local programs servicing battered women and their children.

Contact:
P.O. Box 18749
Denver, CO 80218-0749
Phone: 303-839-1852
www.webmerchants.com/ncadv

Polly's Place Network

Polly's Place Network was founded to provide financial support, consultation, education, evaluation and research in family violence, related abuse and teen pregnancy for Polly's Place programs, churhes, schools and other organizations. PPN is a non-profit affiliated with the Upper Columbia Conference Corporation of Seventh-day Adventists. The network utilizes campetent and dedicated individuals to conduct educational programs, workshops, seminars, presentations, provide research information, etc. Contact us to learn more about our affiliate programs and services at:

P.O. Box 19039
Spokane, WA 99219-9039
Phone: (509) 838-2761
Email: pollysplacenetwork@uccsda.org
www.pollysplacenetwork.org

Women & Men Against Sexual Harassment & Other Abuses (W.A.S.H.)

W.A.S.H. is committed to cultivating healing environments in the family, church and church-related workplaces to restore both victims and perpetrators of sexual, physical and emotional abuse.

Contact:
4309 Sandy Spring Road
Burtonsville, MD 20866-1139
Phone: 800-433-9274 or 301-384-3727
www.tagnet.org/wash

Mable C. Dunbar, Ph. D. is founder of Women In Renewal, Inc., and Polly's Place Ministries, nonprofit organizations that provide a Christian response to domestic violence; Women's Ministries Director, and Family Life Educator for the Upper Columbia Conference of Seventh-day Adventists. She also maintains a private consulting and counseling practice in Spokane, WA. She has a Ph. D. degree in Family Mediation, Master of Arts Degree in Educational & Counseling Psychology, is a Licensed Professional Counselor, Certified Cognitive/Behavioral Therapist, and Certified Domestic Violence Counselor. Mable also conducts workshops and seminars on a national as well as international basis on domestic violence, marriage and family issues, and women's issues.